Times and Seasons

God's Plan for History

Ron McKenzie

Kingwatch Books

Kingwatch Books
Christchurch
New Zealand
www.kingwatch.co.nz

Contents

Warning

This book takes a very different approach to God's plan for history. Before beginning to read it, you will need to set aside much of the stuff that you have learned from the end-time teachers. If you cling to traditional teaching about the seven-year tribulation, the rapture and the millennium, you will not be able to understand the message of this book. If you can leave these things behind, you will discover that God has an amazing plan for this world, far greater than anything ever dreamed of by the end-time prophets.

Keywords

This book cannot contain all that could be written on this topic. On pages where a keyword is listed, more information can be read by going to www.kingwatch.co.nz/keywords.htm and clicking on the appropriate keyword.

Arrows

To assist readers, an arrow at the beginning of each chapter points to the part of the diagram on page 8 that is being covered.

1
Change of Season

End of the World?

Many Christians believe that we are getting close to the second coming of Jesus. Those who believe that the end of the world is near assume that we have entered the "end times" or "last days". They are right to think that we are getting close to a change of season, but because they do not understand the times and seasons, they are looking for the wrong events (keyword: Wheat and Tares).

Most Christians assume that God's plan has the following steps.

Jesus ministry ▶ Church age ▶ End times ▶ End of World

This outline is wrong. It has caused widespread confusion.

Firstly, the end of the world is not the next big event on God's timetable. He has many things to do before his plans for this earth are complete, so the end of the world is a long way off. Other epochal events are more important and much closer.

Secondly, the expression "end times" is not used in the scriptures. Seeking the "end times" is a distraction that has prevented God's people from understanding his plans.

Seasons and Epochs

God is working out his plan for history. The rising and falling of the nations are fixed in his plan.

> He marked out their appointed times in history and the boundaries of their lands (Acts 17:26).

God knows the beginning from the end. To shape events on earth, he had divided history into seasons and determined what will happen in each one. God expects his people to know his plans and understand what he is doing in each season (1 Thes 5:1).

The word "epoch" is derived from a Greek word, which means "pause". It was often used to describe the breaks between the acts of a play. In God's plan, each new season is started by an epochal event that marks the end of the old season and the beginning of the next. God breaks in to changes the "state of play."

The key epochal events in the Old Testament were the creation, the fall, the flood, the tower of Babel, the exodus, the kingship of David, the exile to Babylon and the return to Israel. In each of these events, God broke into history and changed the situation on earth. The ministry of Jesus was the ultimate epochal event that marked the beginning of the New Testament era. We should understand the times and seasons that were set into play by Jesus' ministry.

Two Halves

Human history since the cross has two parts. During the first half, the church struggles to have an impact on the world. During the second half, the Kingdom of God grows to fulfilment and fills the earth with the glory of God. Jesus does not return at the end of the first half. He returns when all God's plans are complete (keyword: Rock and Mountain).

The first half of the New Testament era began with the Last Days of the Jewish religious system. This short season ended with the Fall of Jerusalem. This serious epochal event opened up the season that Jesus called the Times of the Gentiles. This long season dominates the first half of the New Testament age.

The end of the Times of the Gentiles is marked by a relatively-short sub-season called the Time of Distress. The Times of the Gentiles and the Time of Distress run in parallel until they both end together.

Last Days ▶ Times of the Gentiles ▶ Time of Distress

The first half of the New Testament age is drawing to a close. The half-time changeover is marked by the Fullness of Israel and the Collapse of Human Government. These epochal events allow the Holy Spirit to kick off a massive Gospel Advance that gives the saints the Kingdom of God. This glorious Kingdom might last on earth for a long time.

The end of the Kingdom season will be marked by another epochal event. A Man of Lawlessness will lead the nations to rebel against God and reject his Kingdom. This Little Season of rebellion will be cut short by Jesus' appearance at the end of history.

Time of Distress ▶ Kingdom of God ▶ Little Season

Five Seasons

The New Testament age consists of five seasons:

1. The Last Days (Heb 1:2)
2. Times of the Gentiles (Luke 21:24)
3. Time of distress(Dan 12:1)
4. Kingdom of God (Luke 11:2; Rev 11:15)
5. Little Season (Rev 20:3).

These seasons vary in length. The first and the last are very short. The second season is much longer. The third is quite short. The fourth will be really long.

The diagram on the next page shows how these seasons and epochal events fit together.

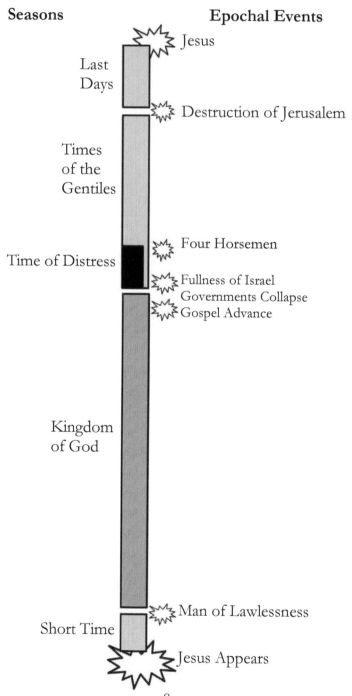

Epochal Events

Nine epochal events mark the transition from one season to another. They are:

- ▶ Jesus Ministry)   to 1
- ▶ Fall of Jerusalem (AD 70)   1 to 2
- ▶ Four Horsemen   to 3
- ▶ Big Battle   ends 3
- ▶ The Fullness of Israel   to 4
- ▶ Collapse of Human Government   to 4
- ▶ Gospel Advance   to 4
- ▶ Man of Lawlessness   4 to 5
- ▶ Jesus Appearance   ends 5.

Where Are We Now?

Many Christians sense that we are coming into a new season, but they misunderstand what this means, because they are confused about the seasons. To know how we should live, we must know what season we are in, and which one comes next. And because the next season is a tough one, we need to know what comes after it, so we do not lose hope.

We are at a pivotal time in human history. The Times of the Gentiles are coming to an end. The reason many Christians feel that the seasons are changing is that we are entering this Time of Distress. This short season runs parallel to the Times of the Gentiles during the final stages of this season. We should be getting ready for this transition.

The Times of the Gentiles and the Time of Distress end together with the Fullness of Israel and The Collapse of Human Government. The Gospel Advance opens the way for the glorious season when the Kingdom of God comes on earth as it is in heaven.

Plenty of Time

Christians are usually in a hurry for the second coming to come. God is gracious, wanting many people to come into his Kingdom, so God is not bound by our sense of urgency.

> With the Lord a day is like a thousand years, and a thousand years are like a day. The Lord is not slow in keeping his promise, as some understand slowness. He is patient with you, not wanting anyone to perish, but everyone to come to repentance (2 Pet 3:8-9).

Using these verses as a key to biblical prophecy misses the point. Peter is explaining that time is different for God. A thousand years seems like a day to him. The two thousand years that have passed since the cross seem like a long time to us, but to God they are just like two days. If only two days have gone by, God has no reason to hurry. He is not slow, but patient. He is willing to let many thousands of years pass so more people can enter his Kingdom.

Christians who want Jesus to return soon are out of touch with God's heart. He did not send his son to die for a handful of people. He is generous and wants hundreds of billions to come into his Kingdom. He would not establish his Kingdom, and then just put it away like last year's toy. If his Kingdom is as glorious as the prophet's promise, he might choose to enjoy it for thousands of years. Here is a woe that should make us worry.

> Woe to those who say, "Let God hurry, let him hasten his work, so we may see it" (Is 5:19).

God is not in a hurry, so his people should be careful about demanding he hurry. He has many unfulfilled promises and needs time to achieve them. We should be as keen as he is to see many billions more people come into the Kingdom.

Those who want to rush Jesus coming do not understand his grace or his concept of time. Ten thousand years are just like a few days to God. We should not be surprised if he chooses to enjoy his Kingdom for thousands of years.

Four to Let Go

To understand God's plan for history, four scriptures that Christians cling to must be taken out of the mix, because they have already been fulfilled. Applying them to the future causes confusion.

1. Jesus Big Prophecy (Matt 24, Mark 13; Luke 21)

This prophecy was fulfilled within the lifetime of those who heard Jesus speak.

> Truly I tell you, this generation will certainly not pass away
> until all these things have happened (Matt 24:34).

Jesus statement is very clear. This message was fulfilled in AD 70, so it should not be used as a prophecy of the future (keyword: Jesus Big Prophecy).

2. The Seventy Weeks of Daniel (Dan 9:20-27)

Daniel was praying for the end of the exile in Babylon. The angel told him what would happen during the next 490 years.

> Seventy 'sevens' are decreed for your people (Dan 9:24).

These 490 years ended with the life of Jesus, so Daniel's prophecy has been fulfilled. Inserting a gap before the last week does not make sense. Pushing this week out into the future produces confusion (keyword: Seventy Sevens).

3. Terrible Times in the Last Days (2 Tim 3:1-5)

A list of sins is used wrongly as a sign of the second coming.

> But mark this: There will be terrible times in the last days
> (2 Tim 3:1).

Paul is warning Timothy to expect hostility from Jewish teachers clinging to their religious system. Timothy had to deal with this stuff, so Paul's warning has already been fulfilled (keyword: Terrible Times).

4. The Woman and the Dragon (Revelation 12)

The book of Revelation covers all of the New Testament. The birth and resurrection of Jesus are described in the vision of the Woman and the Dragon.

> Her child was snatched up to God and to his throne (Rev 12:5).

The vision ends with Israel being scattered among the nations by the Roman Empire. Christians have confused themselves by applying this passage to the future (keyword: Woman and Dragon).

These four passages are favourites with Christians who want to understand the future, but they have been fulfilled already, so we must let them go. We do not lose anything by this, as there are plenty of prophetic passages waiting for fulfilment. Those who want to understand God's plan for history should focus on scriptures that have not been fulfilled. As long as we keep pushing scriptures that have already been fulfilled into the future, confusion will abound.

2

The Book of Revelation

Most Christians understand the book of Revelation as a timeline of events leading up to the second coming. This is a serious mistake. Revelation covers the whole of New Testament history, but focuses intensely on the middle of the diagram on page 8 by explaining how the judgments of God, tribulation and suffering fit together with the collapse of human government, the calling of the Jews and the coming of the Kingdom. The main themes are listed in the prologue.

1. Destruction of Human Political Power

Jesus greets the churches as the ruler of all kings.

> Jesus Christ, the faithful witness, the firstborn from the dead, and the ruler over the kings of the earth (Rev 1:5).

Jesus is the ruler of the kings of the earth. This gives kings and political leaders two choices. If they oppose Jesus, they will be swept away by judgement. If they acknowledge Jesus as Lord, they will have to step down from their positions of power, as a kingdom cannot have two kings.

2. Judgment

Jesus will send judgment on those who oppose him.

> Look he is coming with the clouds and all the peoples of the earth will mourn because of him (Rev 1:7).

The expression "coming on the clouds" is not a description of the second coming, but an Old Testament expression referring to any manifestation in history of God's omnipotent power against the world. The Greek word translated "coming" is "erchomai", the normal word for come. "Parousia", which is used throughout the New Testament for the Appearance of Jesus, is not used in the book of Revelation, because the second coming is not a major theme.

3. Fullness of the Jews
John describes a time when Israel comes to faith in Jesus.
> Every eye will see him, even those who pierced him (Rev 1:7).

In contrast with many other verses that speak of people seeing Jesus, this one includes "those who pierced him". As part of a worldwide move of the Holy Spirit, the Jews will come to faith in Christ. The eyes of their hearts will be opened to see Jesus and accept him as their Saviour.

4. Trouble and Distress
John himself was going through a time of trouble when he received this vision.
> I John, your brother and companion in the suffering and kingdom and patient endurance that are ours in Jesus, was on the island of Patmos because of the word of God and the testimony of Jesus (Rev 1:9).

John encourages Christians to persevere and endure patiently through trouble and distress.

5. Suffering
Suffering brings in the Kingdom.
> I, John, your brother and companion in the suffering and kingdom and patient endurance that are ours in Jesus (Rev 1:9).

The Kingdom does not come when Christians gain political power. As Christians follow Jesus example and take up the cross of suffering, the political powers will collapse, allowing the Kingdom to emerge.

6. Kingdom of God

The Kingdom of God is the central theme in the book of Revelation.

> He has made us kings and priests to His God and Father,
> to Him be glory and dominion forever and ever. Amen
> (Rev 1:6).

The Old Testament prophesied the Kingdom of God. Jesus said it was near. The book of Revelation explains how the Kingdom of God comes to fulfilment on earth.

7. Sovereignty

The sovereignty of Jesus is emphasised throughout Revelation.

> I am the Alpha and the Omega, who is and who was, and
> who is to come, the Almighty (Rev 1:8).

Jesus has existed from the beginning, and he will be in control at the end. Because he is eternal, he knows all things. He is almighty, so he can do all things. His authority and sovereignty are absolute and total.

8. Not Heaven

John records several different visions of the heavenly realms. Many Christians assume these are descriptions of eternal life at the end of the age, but this is not true. Revelation describes things in heaven that God wants to bring to pass on earth. It has little to say about our future life.

Structure of the Book

The Book of Revelation is dominated by the ascension of Jesus. There is a vision of the ascension at the beginning (Rev 4,5), in the middle (Rev 12) and the end of the book (Rev 20). Each of these visions is followed by a description of the outworking of the ascension in human history.

John's vision is shaped by sevens, including seven seals, seven trumpets and seven bowls. Many commentators treat these sets of sevens as sequential, but this leads to confusion.

The sets of seven run in parallel, but each seven develops the events described in the previous one.

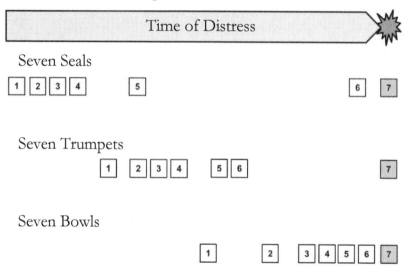

The sevens describe the Time of Distress at the end of the Times of the Gentiles. Each of the sevens ends with the release of the Kingdom of God.

The first four seals describe the beginning of the Time of Distress (Rev 6:1-8). A seal is a mark of ownership. The seven seals (Rev 6) are a set of events that God will use to purify and refine his people. The seals are opened by Jesus in response to the prayers of the saints (Rev 5:8). The seventh seal brings the fulfilment of the Kingdom (Rev 8:1).

The seven trumpets are concentrated in the middle of the Time of Distress when the season is building to a climax. Trumpets are a warning of judgment (Amos 3:6-7; Is 18:3). They are launched by the prayers of the saints (Rev 8:3-5) and they call the church to action. The seventh trumpet releases the fulfilment of the Kingdom.

> The kingdom of the world has become
> the kingdom of our Lord and of his Messiah,
> and he will reign for ever and ever (Rev 11:15).

The seven thunders were sealed up (Rev 10:3-4). They would have extended the judgment, but God cut the Time of Distress short, because he is merciful.

The seven bowls are concentrated at the end of the Time of Distress. They bring the destruction of human governments and deliverance for the people of God, just as the ten plagues destroyed the armies of Pharaoh and freed the children of Israel to enter the promised land. The seventh bowl releases the destruction of human government, which enables the Kingdom of God to emerge on earth.

Seeing the Spiritual Dimension

We usually think of heaven and earth as two different places. Heaven is up there and earth is down here, with a huge gap in between. The boundary is real, but they are not as separate as we assume. We live in a multi-dimensional universe in which the spiritual dimensions exist in parallel to the three-dimensional physical world. Angels can move between the spiritual and physical dimensions, but humans only see the physical side of existence.

Prior to the fall, Adam and Eve could see into the spiritual realms, so they were aware of God walking in the garden. When they sinned, they lost this ability. Human eyes are now so focussed on the physical world that we often misunderstand what is happening around us. Paul explained,

> Our struggle is not against flesh and blood, but against the rulers, against the authorities, against the powers of this dark world and against the spiritual forces of evil in the heavenly realms (Eph 6:12).

If we could see more clearly, we would have a better understanding of Jesus victory. When we were baptised into him, we died with him and rose to sit with him at the right hand of the father in heaven.

> God raised us up with Christ and seated us with him in the heavenly realms in Christ Jesus (Eph 2:6).

If we could see into the spiritual realms, we would see ourselves sitting in the presence of the Father surrounded by millions of angels. This would give us huge confidence during the trials of life. When Elisha opened the eyes of his servant to see the spiritual armies fighting for Israel, his view of the battle was totally changed (2 Kings 6:17). Daniel's faith increased when he realised that geopolitical events were the outcome of a struggle between a few big angels (Dan 10).

When we are born again of the Spirit, our ability to see into the spiritual world is partially restored. Paul prayed that the Ephesians would gain more insight into the spiritual realms (Eph 1:18). As we walk in the Spirit and grow in faith, our insight into the spiritual realms should increase, but it will never be complete.

> For we know in part and we prophesy in part. But when that which is perfect has come, then that which is in part will be done away (1 Cor 13:9-10).

This side of the final resurrection, we never have a totally clear view of the spiritual realms, so people with prophetic insight have an important role in explaining the link between events in the spiritual realms and those on earth.

When his life was drawing to a close, John was given a unique ability to see into the spiritual realms.

> The revelation from Jesus Christ, which God gave him to show his servants (Rev 1:1).

The Greek word translated "revelation" is "apokalupsis". It means unveiling or uncovering. Our focus on the physical dimensions of life hides the spiritual dimensions and gives us a false view of reality. The spiritual world was unveiled for John and he got a glimpse of reality as the angels see it. Jesus gave him this revelation to show that our view of reality is only half the truth (keyword: Spiritual or Literal).

The world assumes that a visionary person sees something that is half real. The truth is opposite. The physical world that we see with our human eyes is only half of reality. The spiritual world unveiled to John in his vision is the other half that we usually miss. John struggled to grasp all that his prophetic eyes saw, but he carefully recorded everything for the benefit of those coming after him. The main purpose of the book of Revelation is to increase our awareness of the spiritual realms. To get a true perspective on reality, we must see things in heaven and things on earth together in Jesus (Eph 1:13). Revelation gives us the other side of reality.

Not What They Seem

John explained that things are not what they seem from the human perspective. The church of Sardis appeared to be strong, but in the spiritual realms, it is very weak.

> I know your deeds; you have a reputation of being alive,
> but you are dead (Rev 3:1).

Military empires may appear invincible to human eyes, but they have already been defeated in the spiritual realms.

A church that is being severely persecuted and is being decimated by political powers looks very different in the spiritual dimensions. To Christians involved in the struggle, the suffering feels intolerable and the gospel seems to be going backwards. In the spiritual realms, these Christians are a mighty army following Jesus to build his Kingdom (keyword: Heavenly Army).

The persecuted church may appear to be weak and helpless, but in the spiritual world, it is preparing to receive the Kingdom (Rev 2:26). When the church is struggling under persecution and the suffering seems intolerable, those who see into the spiritual dimensions will realise that they are close to victory over the forces of the world (Rev 19:14). John's vision of the spiritual realms casts events on earth in a fresh light that gives Christians new hope.

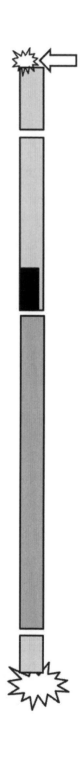

3
Jesus Ministry

Beauty Destroyed

God created a beautiful world in a wonderful universe. For some reason we do not understand, a revolt ruptured the spiritual realms and a third of the angels rebelled against God's plans. This mutiny had immediate impact on earth. Adam and Eve gave in to temptation, so sin and evil took hold on earth.

Sin changed everything.

- The universe was contaminated.
- The earth was corrupted.
- Earthquakes, volcanoes, hurricanes and storms wreaked destruction.
- Horrible weeds spread throughout the earth.
- Animal life was transformed.
- Some animals became violent and dangerous.
- Growing food became hard work.
- Humans lost their communion with God.
- People closed off from each other.
- Evil spirits invaded the world.

- Sickness and disease became normal.
- Death became painful and distressing.
- Evil gained control of the world.
- Fear and anger spread.
- Political powers emerged in efforts to restrain evil.

God's beautiful world was totally stuffed up.

Jesus is the Man

In the fullness of time, Jesus left his home in the spiritual realms, was born as baby and grew to be a man. He began his ministry by pushing back against the evil that had contaminated the earth.

- Healed the sick;
- Cast out evil spirits;
- Built relationships with his disciples;
- Fed the hungry;
- Raised the dead;
- Calmed the storm;
- Challenged the political powers;
- And more....

At the climax of his ministry, Jesus was killed on the cross. What seemed like defeat was actually a tremendous victory over sin and evil.

- Jesus death paid the penalty for sin.
- Every person born on earth can be set free from sin.
- Forgiveness is freely available through faith.
- Jesus rose from the dead making new life available to all people.
- All who believe can be born again into a new life.
- The Holy Spirit was poured out to empower believers.
- The Kingdom of God was inaugurated on earth.

Evil Defeated

Jesus ministry on earth was the greatest epochal event that will ever occur. Sin had given the devil and his evil powers authority on earth. Jesus death destroyed that authority.

> He too shared in their humanity so that by his death he might destroy him who holds the power of death—that is, the devil (Heb 2:14).

Sin and evil had come into the world though human disobedience, so only a human could push them out again. By becoming a man and paying the penalty for sin, Jesus destroyed the power of evil.

> He forgave us all our sins, having cancelled the written code…that stood opposed to us; he took it away, nailing it to the cross. And having disarmed the powers and authorities, he made a public spectacle of them, triumphing over them by the cross (Col 2:13-15).

Human sin had empowered the spiritual forces of wickedness. Jesus death and resurrection destroyed this power. Since the cross, the principalities and powers have hung round on earth getting into mischief, but their status has changed. They are now imposters and trespassers in Jesus' world, waiting nervously for his disciples to expose them and push them out. Jesus death and resurrection were an enormous setback for the powers of evil. If Christians understood this victory, evil would have been squeezed out of the world by now.

Work Complete

As his life ebbed away, Jesus gasped his final words, "It is finished". He was not speaking of his pain, but declaring that his work on earth was finished, forever. He does not have to return to earth at the end of the age to get the job done. He has done everything that he had to do to bring in the Kingdom of God. His work is complete.

When he ascended into heaven, Jesus handed responsibility for establishing the Kingdom over to the Holy

Spirit. He sent him into the world to clean up the mess of sin and bring in the Kingdom. Jesus had established the spiritual victory, so he sent the Spirit to make this victory real on earth. Peter explained this on the Day of Pentecost.

> God has raised this Jesus to life, and we are all witnesses of it. Exalted to the right hand of God, he has received from the Father the promised Holy Spirit and has poured out what you now see and hear (Acts 2:32-33).

Jesus was exalted to the right hand of God, where he received the Holy Spirit and sent him into the world to establish the Kingdom.

Peter quoted Psalm 110:1 to explain why.

> The Lord says to my lord:
> "Sit at my right hand
> until I make your enemies
> a footstool for your feet."

The Father did not tell Jesus to sit at his right hand until it is time to return to earth to defeat his enemies and establish the Kingdom. He told Jesus to remain seated until this task is complete. Returning to the earth to defeat his enemies and establish the Kingdom is not something that God expects of Jesus.

The Holy Spirit is the Kingdom Builder

The humanness that enabled Jesus to win victory on the cross makes it impossible for him to implement that victory on earth. Too put evil back in its place, he would have to operate everywhere on earth instantly, but he cannot do that because he is confined to a human body.

The Holy Spirit is the perfect person for this role. He could not die on the cross, because he does not have a human body, but because he is spirit, he can be active all over the earth at any time. The Holy Spirit is better equipped to build the Kingdom on earth than Jesus. This is why Jesus said it was better for him to go away and let the Holy Spirit come.

> It is to your advantage that I go away; for if I do not go
> away, the Helper will not come to you; but if I depart, I
> will send Him to you (John 16:7).

Jesus was glad to send the Holy Spirit, because he knew that he can establish the Kingdom. The Holy Spirit can convict the people of the world of guilt and sin. He has the ability to bring every person on the earth to faith in Jesus. All he needs is the freedom to act and a body to carry him into the world where he can flow out and touch those who need him.

Jesus does not seek his own glory. He is glad to stand aside and work through the Holy Spirit in the current age. The Holy Spirit can do greater things than Jesus did (John 14:12). He is not confined by time and place, so he can extend the influence of Jesus though the entire earth.

Jesus ministry on earth was the most important event in human history. Not only did he deal with sin and evil, he also released the Holy Spirit on earth to be the Kingdom builder. The Holy Spirit is now at work rolling back all the harm done by sin and evil.

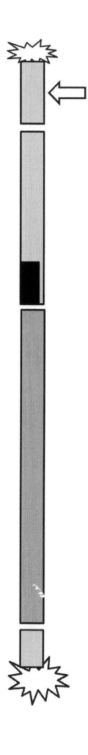

4

Last Days

A new season called the last days began when Jesus arrived on earth.

> God, who at various times and in various ways spoke in time past to the fathers by the prophets, has in these *last days* spoken to us by his Son whom He has appointed heir of all things (Heb 1:1-2).

The Last Days ended with the destruction of Jerusalem in AD 70. During this short season, the Jewish religious system ground to a halt.

Old Order Gone

The letter to the Hebrews explains that the temple sacrifices only applied until the new order was established by Jesus.

> The gifts and sacrifices being offered were not able to clear the conscience of the worshiper. They are only… external regulations applying until the time of the new order (Heb 9:9-10).

The death and resurrection of Jesus marked the end of the old system and the beginning of a new order. Jesus ministry was the epochal event that brought in the Last Days of the Old Testament system. It struggled on for a while, but its days were numbered.

Jesus ministry ended God's purposes for Jerusalem.

- The temple in Jerusalem had been the centre of sacrifice; but Jesus death on the cross put an end to sacrifice forever, so animal sacrifices in an earthly temple were redundant. Jesus became the true high priest, so the Jewish priests were redundant.
- Jerusalem had been the throne of the King of Israel. When Jesus ascended to the right hand of the Father, he was crowned as King of Kings and Lord of Lords. Any role for the king of Israel was gone.

When Jesus entered the presence of God as the perfect High Priest and was appointed as King of Creation, the old order was finished.

God sent the Holy Spirit into the church to do his work in the world.

> He has made us to be a kingdom and priests to serve his God and Father (Rev 1:6).

The body of Christ became the kings and priests who serve God in the world, making the old order redundant. It carried on as if nothing had happened, but it was in its Last Days.

Confusion

Many readers will find it hard to believe that the "last days" are finished. The reason for the muddle is that the last days (plural) of the Jewish system are confused with the last day (singular), the glorious day when Jesus will appear. The Last Days are the period of time between the ministry of Jesus and the destruction of Jerusalem in AD 70. The Last Day is the day when Jesus appears. The former is a season, whereas the latter is an epochal event.

The New Testament has only five references to the last days (Acts 2:17; 2 Tim 3:1; Heb 1:2; James 5:3; 2 Pet 3:3) and two referring to the last times (1 Pet 1:20; Jude 18). James and Peter's letters were written to Jewish Christians. Hebrews was a letter to all Jews. Timothy was a Jew. This means that all New Testament references to the last days are in epistles written to Jews. They would have understood that they were living in the last days of their national system. This is why four of the seven authors wrote they were living in the last days (eg Heb 1:2).

Mercy

The Last Days were not important for the Gentiles, except that Jesus opened the gospel to everyone on earth.

> The gospel is bearing fruit and growing throughout the whole world (Col 1:6).

The Last Days were a season of mercy for Israel. This short season gave all the adults who were present when Jesus was crucified a chance to change their attitude to him. Anyone who was an adult in AD 33 when Jesus died would be quite old by AD 70 when the Last Days came to an end. The season of mercy gave them the remainder of their lives to admit they were wrong and make peace with God.

Jesus had prophesied that the religious and political leaders of Israel would continue to reject him (Matt 23:33-39), but God is always fair, so he gave them plenty of time to acknowledge Jesus as their messiah. Nearly forty years would pass before their fate was set in stone. Unfortunately, this season of mercy was mostly wasted.

What should have happened? When Jesus died on the cross, the Jewish leaders should have put a stop to the sacrifices in the temple. These had always pointed forward to Jesus, so once he had died, they were obsolete. When Jesus ascended and was ordained as the perfect high priest, the priests in Jerusalem should have resigned and gone home. Once the Holy Spirit had been poured out at Pentecost, every believer becomes a temple of the Holy Spirit, so there was no need for a special building for God to dwell in. The temple in Jerusalem was made irrelevant, so it should have been turned into a museum or art gallery.

The priests and political leaders were so attached to their old order that they could not let it go. They continued to offer animal sacrifices in the temple. These offerings could not point to Jesus anymore, so they became a blasphemous insult against him. Priests continuing in their role became usurpers of Jesus ministry. They should have put their robes away and gone out to preach the good news. Worse still, the Jewish leaders attacked the fledgling church. Throughout the Acts of the Apostles, the most serious persecution came from the Jewish leaders.

The gospel was preached throughout Israel during the Last Days, but most of the people hardened their hearts.

> What the people of Israel sought so earnestly they did not obtain. The elect among them did, but the others were hardened (Rom 11:7).

The Jews did not take advantage of the mercy shown them during the Last Days of the old order, so God had no option but to bring the temple system to an end and scatter the people among the nations.

New Covenant

The covenant of Moses had become a burden for the people of Israel. It promised great blessings, but they were unable to receive them, because their covenant was too hard to fulfil. Their disobedience constantly put them on the wrong side of their covenant under its curses.

Jesus fulfilled the covenant on behalf of everyone united with him by faith. His new covenant opened the way for Israel to fulfil the old covenant. Israel had a wonderful covenant, but they rejected the one who enabled them to fulfil it. Without a covenant with Jesus, the covenant with Moses was valid, but deficient. If they had accepted Jesus, Israel would have been able to fulfil their covenant by faith and receive the promised blessings.

Summary

- The Last Days began with Jesus ministry on earth.

  In these last days he has spoken to us by his Son,
  whom he appointed heir of all things (Heb 1:2).

  He was chosen before the creation of the world, but was
  revealed in these last times for your sake (1 Pet 1:20).

- The Last Days really kicked in when the Holy Spirit
  was poured out on all believers at Pentecost.

  No, this is what was spoken by the prophet Joel:
  In the last days, God says,
  I will pour out my Spirit on all people (Acts 2:16-17).

- The gospel was preached to the Jews during the last
  days.

- The Last Days were a season of mercy that gave those
  who had refused to accept Jesus as their Messiah an
  opportunity to change their minds.

- Most of the Jewish people hardened their hearts against
  the gospel. Many would scoff at the gospel.

  You must understand that in the last days scoffers will
  come, scoffing and following their own evil desires (2
  Pet 3:3).

  In the last times there will be scoffers who will follow
  their own ungodly desires (Jude 18).

- The gospel was taken into all the world.

  The gospel is bearing fruit and growing throughout the
  whole world—just as it has been doing among you
  since the day you heard it (Col 1:6).

- The Jews persecuted those who preached the gospel.

  Jews who refused to believe stirred up the other
  Gentiles and poisoned their minds against the brothers
  (Acts 14:2).

- The Last Days lasted for forty years.

- The Last Days ended when Jerusalem was destroyed in
  AD 70.

▶ Destruction of Jerusalem

The epochal event that marked the end of the Last Days and the beginning of the next season is the Destruction of Jerusalem. When the temple was destroyed and the Jewish people scattered into exile, the old order that had obstinately persisted on throughout the Last Days was finally dead. The destruction of Jerusalem was the final 'nail in the coffin' of the old system.

Jesus predicted the fall of Jerusalem in Matthew 24:1-35, Mark 13:1-31 and Luke 21:5-33. Most Christians believe these verses describe events before the second coming, but this is wrong. To understand these verses, we must note the question that Jesus was answering. The disciples had commented on the glory and beauty of the temple.

> Some of his disciples were remarking about how the temple was adorned with beautiful stones and with gifts dedicated to God. But Jesus said, "As for what you see here, the time will come when not one stone will be left on another; every one of them will be thrown down" (Luke 21:5-6).

Jesus warned that the temple would be totally destroyed. The disciples could not believe his words, because the temple was the centre of their world, so they asked him when these things would happen. Jesus gave them the signs leading up to this terrible event (keyword: Jesus Big Prophecy).

He warned Christians to flee Jerusalem when it was surrounded by armies.

> When you see Jerusalem being surrounded by armies, you will know that its desolation is near. Then let those who are in Judea flee to the mountains, let those in the city get out, and let those in the country not enter the city.... For this is the time of punishment in fulfilment of all that has been written. How dreadful it will be in those days for pregnant women and nursing mothers! There will be great distress in the land and wrath against this people. They will fall by the sword and will be taken as prisoners to all

> the nations. Jerusalem will be trampled on by the Gentiles
> until the times of the Gentiles are fulfilled (Luke 21:20-23).

In AD 70, a Roman army surrounded Jerusalem and started a terrible siege. The Jewish historian Josephus described the siege and the terrible tribulation it caused. Conditions were so severe that mothers ate their babies to survive. Jesus' awful prophecies were fulfilled. Christians who had heeded Jesus warning left the city before the siege began and fled to the safety of the mountains.

The Destruction of Jerusalem was the epochal event that marked the beginning of a new season called the Times of the Gentiles. It was a judgment event for Israel.

> For this is the time of punishment in fulfilment of all that
> has been written (Luke 21:22).

Forty years after the Jews had rejected Jesus, the Romans destroyed Jerusalem and the Jews were scattered among the nations. The destruction of Jerusalem was a judgment on the city that had crucified the Son of God and rejected his ministry.

The destruction of Jerusalem brought dramatic change to the church. During the Last Days, the fledging church was centred on Jerusalem. Once the city was destroyed, its centre of gravity shifted to Asia Minor.

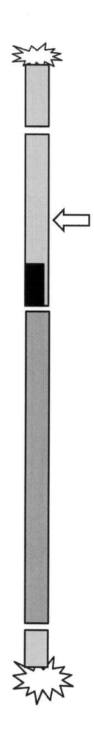

5

The Times of the Gentiles

Jesus named the season following the Last Days when he prophesied the destruction of Jerusalem.

> Jerusalem will be trampled on by the Gentiles until the
> **Times of the Gentiles** are fulfilled (Luke 21:24).

Jesus called this season the "Times of the Gentiles", because it is defined by Jerusalem being trampled by the nations.

In the previous verses, Jesus clearly described the epochal event that would begin the Times of the Gentiles.

> There will be great distress in the land and wrath against
> this people. They will fall by the sword and will be taken
> as prisoners to all the nations (Luke 21:23-24).

The Roman armies invaded Israel and destroyed Jerusalem in AD 70. The Jewish people were taken prisoner and scattered among the nations. This event marked the beginning of the Times of the Gentiles. The epochal event that ends this season has not yet occurred, so we are still living in the season called the Times of the Gentiles. Paul gives the reason for the season in his letter to the Romans.

> Israel has experienced a hardening in part until the fullness
> of the Gentiles has come in (Rom 11:25).

During the Times of the Gentiles, most Jews are hardened to the gospel, the church is dominated by gentile Christians and

Jerusalem is ruled by gentile armies. Only a few Jews can find peace through Jesus and Jerusalem has no peace.

Paul describes Israel as a disobedient nation (Rom 10:21). Although a few have been saved, the nation as a whole is shut off from God. They are enemies of the gospel (Rom 11:28) committed to disobedience (Rom 11:31) and broken off the vine (Rom 11:17).

During the Times of the Gentiles, the majority of Jews are absent from the Kingdom, because their nation has rejected their messiah and is under judgment. The Kingdom cannot come to fulfilment until the judgment of Israel is complete.

Power to the Enemy
This disobedience has consequences throughout the world. When Jesus died upon the cross, the devil was totally and fully defeated. He was cast out of heaven and can only continue to function on earth, if he can deceive people into rejecting the gospel (Rev 12:13). However, he does have one last legal right on earth. The spiritual status of the Jews gives Satan the right to do evil against them (Matt 23:39).

Since the Jews had been scattered among the nations, he has been able to work in most nations. Whenever Satan wants to do great evil in a nation, he incites it to attack the Jews and then he has greater authority to do harm. For example, Satan incited both Hitler and Stalin to attack the Jews, which allowed him to do great evil through these men.

Character of the Season
During the Times of the Gentiles:
- The Jews are scattered among the nations for their safety.
- They continue to resist the gospel.
- Evil is unrestrained
- The world is dominated by political power.

- Human government is unrestrained.
- The church is constrained by lack of faith.
- The Holy Spirit is restrained, because he will not go where he is not invited.

This is why the battle has been so hard for the last two millennia. Part of the team is missing. The church is not complete, so it has been operating at half power.

Time Times and Half a Time

A phrase used several times in Revelation and Daniel to mark out this season is "a time, times and half a time". This phrase is essential for the understanding the Times of the Gentiles. The interpretation is quite simple.

$$a \text{ time} = \text{one year},$$

$$\text{times} = \text{two years}$$

$$\text{half a time} = \text{half a year}$$

This means that "a time, times and half a time" equals three and a half years:

$$3\frac{1}{2} \text{ years} = \text{time, times and a half}$$

Daniel and Revelation use two other expressions in a similar way. Three and half years is the same as forty-two months:

$$12 \times 3\frac{1}{2} = 42$$

In the Hebrew calendar, a month is thirty days, so three and a half years equals 1,260 days.

$$12 \times 30 \times 3\frac{1}{2} = 1260$$

The key to interpreting these expressions is to understand that the New Testament age has two halves. Three and half is half of seven. Seven signifies fullness or perfection, so seven years represent the entire New Testament age, from the ascension of Jesus to the end of the age. These seven years can be split into two halves. The following expressions for "three and half years" in Revelation and Daniel refer to the Times of the Gentiles, which is the first half of the New Testament age;

- time, times and half a time;
- 1260 days;
- forty-two months;
- three and half years;
- Times of the Gentiles.

Two Lampstands

In a vision of two lampstands, John was given a rod to measure the temple of God and count the worshippers.

> Exclude the outer court; do not measure it, because it has been given to the Gentiles. They will trample on the holy city for **42 months** (Rev 11:2).

The temple was the dwelling place of God. Those who enter the courts of the temple have access to the presence of God. The Gentiles will dominate access to God for forty-two months. During this season, the Jewish people are shut out from the presence of God (but kept safe by being scattered among the nations).

The forty-two months represents the first half of the New Testament age, when the gospel goes out to the Gentiles. Most of the Jewish people will be unable to receive the gospel because their hearts are hardened. They are reluctant to recognise Jesus as their messiah, so the church is filled up with Gentiles. The Gentile nations dominate the world.

Truncated Church

John saw two witnesses, two olive trees and two lampstands.

> And I will give power to my two witnesses, and they will prophesy for **1,260 days**, clothed in sackcloth. These are the two olive trees and the two lampstands that stand before the Lord of the earth (Rev 11:3-4).

The lampstands and the witnesses represent the church. It is Jesus witness in the world. The olive trees represent the Holy Spirit. The odd thing in this vision is that there are only two lampstands. Earlier John had seen seven lamp-stands.

> The mystery of the seven stars that you saw in my right hand and of the seven golden lampstands is this: The seven stars are the angels of the seven churches, and the seven lampstands are the seven churches (Rev 1:20).

Seven represents perfection or completion. The perfected, completed church is represented by seven lampstands. A church with only two lampstands is a truncated church that cannot provide a complete witness to Jesus.

The church is truncated because the Jewish people are missing. A church without the chosen people is incomplete. With part of the team missing, the church is ineffective. This truncated church is active for 1260 day, which is the Times of the Gentiles. John is explaining that the church will not reach its full potential during the first half of its history, because the Jews are missing. That has been the story for the last two thousand years.

The two olive trees represent a constrained Holy Spirit. A perfectly free Holy Spirit would be represented by seven olive trees. During the season represented by the 1260 days, the Holy Spirit will be constrained by lack of faith in the church, and be unable to operate to his full potential. When this season ends, the Holy Spirit will be able to speak and act effectively on earth.

Political Power

The truncated church uses Old Testament methods, because it does not fully understand the calling of the cross.

> If anyone tries to harm them, fire comes from their mouths and devours their enemies. This is how anyone who wants to harm them must die (Rev 11:5).

This points to Elijah, who called down fire on the soldiers who had tracked him down (2 Kings 1:9-15). Elijah tried to control the world using spiritual power, but his strategy failed and he had to flee. Power without suffering always fails.

During the Times of the Gentiles, the church uses spiritual power to control the political powers, in the same way that Elijah attempted to control King Ahab. It tries to advance the Kingdom of God by imposing Christian laws on the rest of society. This strategy fails, because God intends his church to pursue the cross, not power.

Israel in Exile

John saw a woman being hidden in the desert during the Times of the Gentiles.

> The woman fled into the desert to a place prepared for her by God, where she might be taken care of for *1,260 days* (Rev 12:6).

> The woman was given the two wings of a great eagle, so that she might fly to the place prepared for her in the desert, where she would be taken care of for a *time, times and half a time*, out of the serpent's reach (Rev 12:14).

The woman in these verses is Israel. John had seen a woman, clothed with the sun, the moon under her feet, and twelve stars on her head. In Joseph's dream, the sun, moon and twelve stars represented his father Jacob (Israel) and his twelve sons, so the woman is Israel (Gen 37:9-10).

This woman was pregnant and gave birth to a male child. This is Jesus, who was born of an Israelite woman in the nation of Israel. John saw the devil attempt to kill the male child, but he was snatched up to heaven (Rev 12:3-5). Satan used Herod in an attempt to destroy Jesus at his birth, but God kept him safe in the desert of Egypt. He also tried to destroy Jesus on the cross, but he was raised into heaven.

After failing to destroy Jesus, the devil turned on the Jewish people. This explains the ferocity of the destruction of Jerusalem in AD 70. The wings of the eagle represent the Roman Empire scattering the Jewish people to the nations across the earth. For people who loved their land, this was like being in "a desert", but it is also a safe place. God keeps his people out of the serpent's reach in exile for the "time, times and half a time" of the Times of the Gentiles.

Powerful Political Power

The Beast of Revelation will be active throughout the Times of the Gentiles.

> The beast was given a mouth to utter proud words and blasphemies and to exercise his authority for **forty-two months** (Rev 13:5).

A beast symbolises human political power. John saw strong human governments exercising authority for forty-two months. Forty-two months is three and half years, so this is the same season. During the times of the Gentiles, this Beast will be active in the world. Human political powers will be so confident that they claim authority that belongs to God.

At the beginning of the Times of the Gentiles, this political power was manifested through the Roman Empire. Towards the end of the season, political dominance will be established through another empire. Daniel saw this terrible beast rising out of the sea. The angel explained.

> After them another king will arise, different from the earlier ones... He will speak against the Most High and oppress his saints and try to change the set times and the laws. The saints will be handed over to him for a time, times and half a time (Dan 7:24-25).

A political empire more powerful and more awful than any that has gone before will emerge in the world. This political power will change laws with total disregard for God's law. It will revolt against God's plans and attempt to accomplish its own goals. This human government will oppress God's people for a time, times and half a time. The Beast will be hanging around in some form or other for the entire season.

Too Long

During the Times of the Gentiles:

- The people of Israel are scattered among the nations.
- They will be hostile to the gospel.
- The church will not reach its full capability.
- The Holy Spirit is constrained.
- Satan has a legal right to be active in the world, despite his defeat.
- The world will be dominated by strong political empires.
- The Kingdom of God rises and declines, but does not come to fulfilment.

The Times of the Gentiles has gone on much longer than God intended, because:

- The people of the world continue to put their faith in political power for security and prosperity.
- Human government is seen as the solution to every problem.
- The Jews continue to resist the idea that Jesus is their messiah.
- Christian witness to the Jews has been defective.
- Christians have been better at persecuting the Jews than demonstrating God's love for them.
- Christians trust in political power, military force and economic riches.
- Christians have encouraged Israeli militarism.
- Most Christians have been unwilling to suffer through a Time of Distress by taking up the cross and following Jesus.

Season End

Jesus explained how to identify the end of the Times of the Gentiles.

> Look, your house is left to you desolate. For I tell you,
> you will not see me again until you say, 'Blessed is he who
> comes in the name of the Lord' (Matt 23:38-39).

The sign that marks the end of the season is Jewish people blessing Christians who have come to share the gospel of Jesus. This has not happened yet, so we are still in the Times of the Gentiles (Blessing Christians is not the same as taking money from Christian nations to buy weapons).

The Times of the Gentiles will end when the sorrows of the Jews are complete. Satan's last legal authority on earth will be gone, so his ability to do evil will be severely curtailed, leading to a rapid decline in evil. Once Satan has lost his right to work in the world, God will be free to pour out his Spirit and bring the Kingdom to its promised fulfilment. The Jews will welcome the gospel and the season of the Kingdom will begin.

Christians often say that God is doing a new thing. We should be careful about making this kind of statement. A new thing will not happen on earth, unless something changes in the spiritual dimension. The ascension of Jesus changed things in heaven, so it resulted in a new thing on earth (Pentecost). Since then, God has mostly been doing the same thing. However, the end of the judgement of Israel does represent a change in the spiritual dimension, so it will produce a "new thing" on earth (Dan 7:26).

The final days of the Times of the Gentiles will be marked by terrible trouble and distress, as the devil strikes out in a last desperate attempt to retain the power that is slipping from his grasp. At the same time, human governments will seize unprecedented political control in order to build paradise on earth. Their efforts will fail dramatically.

The Time of Distress is a sub-season that runs in parallel with Times of the Gentiles. These seasons end together with the Fullness of Israel.

▶ The Four Horsemen

The epochal event that marks the beginning of the Time of Distress is the release of the Four Horseman of Revelation 6. We are now well through the Times of the Gentiles and beginning the Time of Distress. The Four Horsemen are the birth pangs of this new season. They are not signs of the second coming or the rapture. They are the events that cause the Time of Distress.

John's vision begins with the opening of a scroll with seven seals. Jesus is the only one who can open the seals. Although these events are unpleasant, they will only come when he is ready. Satan has no authority to bring them to pass. These events are initiated in heaven, so they will bring blessing to God's people.

As each seal was opened, John saw a horseman ride forth. Each horseman represents an actor in human history that causes a decisive event. These events follow on from each other, but also overlap each other.

Zechariah 6:1-8 records a parallel vision of four chariots coming out from between two mountains. He does not tell us what each one does, but he indicates the direction they go.

The White Horse

When the first seal was opened, a bowman on the white horse rode out.

> Before me was a white horse! Its rider held a bow, and he was given a crown, and he rode out as a conqueror bent on conquest (Rev 6:2).

The rider looks like Jesus, because he rides on a white horse, but Jesus is armed with a sword, so this is not him. This bowman represents a false messiah or a false religion making a powerful advance (Ps 46:9).

Several Old Testament nations are described as bowmen. Elam, which was situated in the western part of modern Iran,

44

is described as armed with a bow (Jer 49:34-39, Is 22:6). The Persian army which came from the same area is described as being armed with bows (Jer 50:14,29,42). Ishmael, was an archer (Gen 21:20). He was the father of the Arab nations, so there are bowmen in Arabia (Is 21:13-16).

The people of Libya are also described as bowmen (Isaiah 66:19). In Jeremiah 46:9, men of Lydia are said to be bowmen. Lydia was situated in modern Turkey. Islam is strong in Iran, Saudi Arabia, Libya and Turkey.

Mohammed is a false prophet who claimed to be the successor to Jesus, so a bowman on a white horse is a good description of the Islamic religion. The white horse going forth "conquering and to conquer" represents the revival of Islamic fervour and political power that has been sweeping the world since the Islamic revolution in Iran in 1978.

Daniel warned that Iran, which was previously called Persia, would push out to the west, the north and the south, and that no nation would be able to stand against it (Dan 8:3-4). Iran has already expanded its influence to the west in Iraq, and to the north in Lebanon and Syria. Its next charge will be south towards Saudi Arabia, which has a tiny population, a significant Shia minority, enormous oil reserves and a massive arsenal of weapons (keyword: Iranian Ram).

The Islamic revival has touched the entire Moslem world. It is very powerful at a grass roots level, and even secular rulers are coming under its influence. Islam has gained influence in the west. This links with Zechariah, who saw white horses advancing to the west (Zech 6:6).

The Red Horse
The second horseman releases ethnic wars across the earth.
> Then another horse came out, a fiery red one. Its rider was given power to take peace from the earth and to make people kill each other. To him was given a large sword (Rev 6:3-4).

A terrible time of war emerges on earth, as men begin to slay each other. The world has experienced war throughout history, but the "large sword" signifies that this time will be different from anything experienced before.

Red is the colour of Esau and the Edomites. Esau was red when he was born (Gen 25:25). His name comes from a root meaning "to press or to squeeze". Esau was told that he would live by the sword (Gen 27:40; Num 20:18). The word Edom, the name of the nation he founded, comes from a root word meaning "red". The life of Esau and the experience of Edom is the key to understanding the rider on the fiery red horse. Their history was a conflict between two families or tribes squeezed together in the same land.

The rider on the fiery red horse represents inter-tribal warfare spreading throughout the world. Tribes that have lived together in an uneasy peace will go to war with each other. Disputes that have festered for hundreds of years will spring to the surface. New generations will turn weapons on their neighbours to settle old grievances. The tribal groups going to war with each other may often be quite closely related. These inter-tribal struggles will be characterised by:

- bitterness (Gen 27:34)
- revenge (Gen 27:41)
- fury (Gen 27:44)
- betrayal (1 Sam 22:9)
- retaliation (Ez 25:12)
- concealment (Jer 49:10)
- lack of wisdom (Jer 49:7)
- rebellion against parents (Gen 28:9)
- grief (Gen 27:35).

These wars will often begin with a guerrilla army fighting against government forces (Gen 25:27). Ruthless fighters will bring great terror on the land (Jer 49:16). Armies will plunder with glee and with malice in their hearts (Ez 36:5), often shedding innocent blood (Joel 3:19). Amos spoke about Edom:

> He pursued his brother with a sword,
> stifling all compassion,
> because his anger raged continually
> and his fury flamed unchecked (Amos 1:10).

The Red Horse has already been at work in Somalia, Bosnia, Kosovo, Rwanda, Sudan, Ireland, Iraq, Sri Lanka, Afghanistan, Azerbaijan, Uzbekistan, Tajikistan, Pakistan and Libya. The revival of Islam feeds these wars in some parts of the world, but Christians are not immune. These ethnic disputes will become so common, that the resources of the United Nations will be unable to cope.

Ethnic disputes are not new. The difference in this season is the ferocity of destruction amplified by modern weapons.

The Black Horse

The third horseman represents a worldwide famine caused by a serious economic collapse.

> Before me was a black horse! Its rider was holding a pair of scales in his hand. Then I heard what sounded like a voice among the four living creatures, saying, "Two pounds of wheat for a day's wages, and six pounds of barley for a day's wages, and do not damage the oil and the wine" (Rev 6:5-6).

The cause of the famine is not explained, but the results are clear. The Greek measure used is a "choinix". It was the daily ration for a soldier on active service. The coin mentioned is a denarius, which was the equivalent of a day's wages. John saw a famine so severe, that a daily ration of wheat will cost a day's wages. Barley was a little cheaper, as it was considered to be of poorer quality. The situation will get so severe that ordinary people have to use all they can earn to buy food. The wealthy will be less affected. Luxury items like oil and wine are not to be damaged.

The main shortage will be basic food items. Zechariah saw black horses moving to the north. In the modern world, the northern nations tend to be wealthy and poorer nations tend to be in the south. John is warning that people in the wealthy nations may experience famine; something they have not known in recent years.

The Pale Horse

The fourth horseman represents epidemic disease and death.

> I looked, and there before me was a pale horse! Its rider was named Death, and Hades was following close behind him (Rev 6:8).

The Greek word is "Thanatos". This word means death, but in the Greek version of the Old Testament, it is used more than thirty times to translate the Hebrew word for "pestilence" (deber), so "pestilence" might be a better translation in this context. This horseman represents deadly disease spreading across the earth. John saw an epidemic like the black death killing people all over the world. It will kill people in four ways.

> They were given power over a fourth of the earth to kill in sword, famine and plague, and by the beasts from the earth (Rev 6:8).

In Revelation, the beasts from the earth represent human political powers. This suggests that these wars, famines and disease will be caused by the actions of human governments.

This horseman was called Pestilence, and Hades follows him. This suggests that those who have rejected the gospel might be more vulnerable. Zechariah saw the pale horse moving south. This suggests that the impact will be worse in the poorer parts of the world.

Four

Four is the number representing the earth, so these events will reach to the four corners of the earth. God promised he would protect his people.

> You will not fear the terror of the night, nor the arrow that flies by day, nor the pestilence that stalks in the darkness, nor the plague that destroys at midday. A thousand may fall at your side, ten thousand at your right hand, but it will not come near you (Ps 91:5-7).

This psalm is a wonderful promise of hope for those who are faithful to the Lord.

A natural connection links the events symbolised by the four horsemen. The first two horsemen open the way for the third and the fourth horsemen. A decline in faith leads to increased warfare. The wasting of war tends to produce death and famine. Shortages of food cause sickness and death. We are seeing the beginnings of these events, but we have certainly not seen their complete fulfilment. Before the first four seals are fulfilled, trouble and distress will sweep the earth on an unprecedented scale.

The Four Horsemen mark the beginning of the Time of Distress. Their activities release the conditions that allow a huge concentration of political and military power. For example, the fear of Islam expanding westward has already led to a big increase in state power and loss of freedom. Fear and uncertainty will bring human political power to a climax, as people give their freedom over to human governments in the hope of finding peace in a troubled world. This has to happen, before faith in human government can be totally broken at the end of the Times of Gentiles and the Time of Distress.

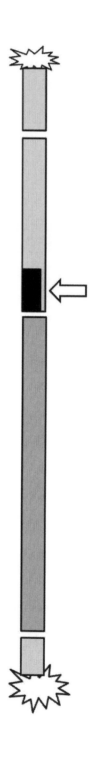

6
Time of Distress

The season that ends the times of the Gentiles is called the Time of Distress. This is the third season following the ministry of Jesus. It will be painful for the world, as troubles and tribulations will break out everywhere. The devil will be angry at losing power, so evil will be rampant.

- Economies will collapse.
- Global trade will contract.
- The division of labour will shrink.
- Wealth will disappear.
- Famine and disaster will be widespread.
- Sickness and disease will be unstoppable.
- Wars will increase in intensity.
- Security structures will fall apart.
- Political power will be concentrated.
- Police and defence forces may not be paid.
- Many will desert their posts.
- Some military leaders will morph into warlords.
- Violent youths will rampage through towns and cities.
- Fear and dread will be pervasive.

The distress will build slowly. Initially, governments will hold back the worst effects, so most people will be confident that the good times will return (keyword: Distress).

Power and Persecution

The Time of Distress will be the last hurrah for human political power. When the troubles begin, governments will grab emergency powers, as their people cry out for relief. Most people will support their leaders' attempts to turn back the tide of evil, so they will deal ruthlessly with those who oppose their increased powers. In many places, governments will be successful in controlling the worst evil, for a while.

As the spirit of fear and dread takes hold, human governments will accrue enormous authority. Political power will be concentrated in the hands of fewer and fewer people.

The principalities and powers will use the Time of Distress to soften up the world for their last power play. When people see their political leaders on television declaring peace and promising to restore broken dreams, their faith in political power will be boosted. Fear of the future and faith in the state are a dangerous mix. When fear and dread are pervasive and faith in human government is widespread, accumulation and concentration of political power is easy.

Many Christians will welcome the expansion of political power as a solution to problems that concern them. A few will see through this accumulation of political power and speak against it. This will lead to the persecution represented by the fifth seal of Revelation.

> When he opened the fifth seal, I saw under the altar the souls of those who had been slain because of the word of God and the testimony they had maintained (Rev 6:9).

Christians exposing their leaders as human messiahs will face terrible persecution.

Political Messiahs

As the Time of Distress progresses, smaller governments will collapse under the strain. Some nations will not be able to cope with the pressure and will go broke. Politicians will feel overwhelmed by troubles and flee from office. Many smaller nations will fall into anarchy, because no one will risk running for office and there is no money to maintain the structures of government. Jeremiah described this time.

> "In that day," declares the Lord, "the king and the officials will lose heart, the priests will be horrified, and the prophets will be appalled" (Jer 4:9).

Difficulties will produce huge disappointment and political leaders will be cursed.

> Distressed and hungry, they will roam through the land; when they are famished, they will become enraged and, looking upward, will curse their king and their God. Then they will look toward the earth and see only distress and darkness and fearful gloom, and they will be thrust into utter darkness (Is 8:21-22).

The situation will be different in larger nations. Local councils and regional governments will grind to a halt, as revenues disappear and politicians bolt from power. People will look to their national and federal governments for deliverance from trouble. Political power will shift from the local to the centre in a last desperate attempt to bring order from the emerging chaos. The larger the nation, the longer political messiahs will be able to hold out by promising deliverance and hope.

We live in a very materialistic age, where people are driven by physical comfort. When difficult times come, most people will submit to political messiahs who promise to restore their affluence. They will sell their freedom for peace and security. These political messiahs will fail, because they are working without God. They will demand huge powers to hold things together, but will make the situation worse.

A great nation will rise up in the west and dominate the world in a desperate attempt to turn back distress. The people of the world will welcome its expanding power, as it intervenes in nasty situations in many places to restore peace and prosperity. The United States is the only western nation with the economic and military strength for this task. More important, it has the democratic credentials and an aspiration to save the world. It is already stepping up to the role.

Democratic Beast

The Beast that emerges during the Time of Distress is very different from previous empires. People will be amazed, because it is a democratic beast.

> The inhabitants of the earth whose names have not been written in the book of life from the creation of the world will be astonished when they see the beast (Rev 17:8).

The distinguishing feature of this empire is that it has died and come back to life.

> One of the heads of the beast seemed to have had a fatal wound, but the fatal wound had been healed. The whole world was astonished and followed the beast (Rev 13:3).

The beast is a form of government that once existed, was destroyed, but will return to dazzle the world.

> The beast, which you saw, once was, now is not, and will come up out of the Abyss and go to his destruction (Rev 17:8).

This form of human government existed before John's time, but had come to such a violent end, that no one expected to see it again. It once existed, it did not exist in John's time, but in the future, it will come back into existence.

> They are also seven kings. Five have fallen, one is, the other has not yet come; but when he does come, he must remain for a little while... The beast who once was, and now is not, is an eighth king. He belongs to the seven and is going to his destruction (Rev 17:10-11).

Rome had a number of different types of government. The key is identifying a form of government that did not exit during John's lifetime, but existed previously. When John was alive, Rome was an empire controlling a large part of the ancient world. This makes the Roman Empire the sixth king. The Beast is a type of government that was brought to a violent end by the Roman Empire.

The major form of human government prior to the Roman Empire was the Roman Republic. It was a copy of the democratic republic that began in Greece much earlier. The Roman Republic began in 500 BC and lasted for nearly five centuries. Consuls were elected for a year. An elected Senate was responsible for passing laws and appointing government officials. Not everyone had the right to vote, but the republic was based on the principle of democracy.

Democracy in Rome came to a violent end about thirty years before Jesus was born. Julius Caesar and his successor Caesar Augustus turned the Roman armies against Rome and destroyed the Republic. By the time Jesus was born, the Empire was fully entrenched in power. Christianity was born when democracy died.

The democratic republic received a fatal blow when Caesar August took control of Rome. "The beast that once was, now is not" is the democratic republic. The beast with the "fatal wound that had been healed" and the "beast who was wounded by the sword and lived" represent the restoration of democratic government in a republic.

John saw the Beast coming out of the sea (Rev 13:1). In Revelation, the sea represents the people of the world.

> Then the angel said to me, "The waters you saw.... are peoples, multitudes, nations and languages" (Rev 17:15).

In most empires, a few powerful men control the people. This beast emerges when people govern themselves. Democracy is the only way a multitude of people can govern themselves. The Beast is a restored democratic republic. Many Christians have been taught that democracy is a Christian form of government. This is not true, as democracy is the opposite of the Kingdom of God. Authority resides with the people in democracy, whereas authority in the Kingdom of God belongs to God.

If a group of people choose to obey God, they will not find his will by voting, but by listening to the Holy Spirit. They may also need prophets to declare his will. Democracy does not lead to the will of God, so it cannot produce his Kingdom. The scriptures show that when the people got to vote, they walked away from God's will.

Democracy is a form of adultery in which people freely surrender to a democratically elected ruler in return for prosperity and security. This adulterous relationship during the Time of Distress makes the Beast different from other empires. Earlier empires killed and stole to provide wealth to the elite. A democratic empire taxes the rich to provide benefits to everyone and attract their votes (keyword: Democratic Beast).

Some Christians believe that the Beast is Islam, but this is not correct. Islam has a big influence during the Time of Distress, but it is not the Beast. The white horse, which represents the advance of Islam, helps create the conditions that open the way for the Beast. It emerges as a solution to the problems caused by the advance of Islam. Islam causes distress whereas the Beast is the great de-stresser.

Widespread Support

The Democratic Beast is different from the empires that have gone before. They were established by military power and anyone who opposed their rule was forced to submit with ruthless violence. The new empire will get its power in a different way.

> He deceives those who dwell on the earth by those signs which he was granted to do in the sight of the beast, telling those who dwell on the earth to make an image to the beast who was wounded by the sword and lived (Rev 13:14).

Instead of being conquered by force, the people of the world will be deceived into free submission. People longing for peace and prosperity will support any government power that promises to fulfil their dreams.

The people of the world will be deceived into supporting this Terrible Beast. Many national leaders will freely submit to the new empire, because it offers military and financial support. This Beast will not rule the world directly, but will extend its influence through subordinate client states.

The only challenge to this aggregation of political power will come from Christians who understand the "signs of the times". When most people are calling on the political powers to do more to turn back the overwhelming crisis, they will expose the real character of the "best government ever". Suggesting that this democratic republic is the next manifestation of the Beast will make them unpopular. Opposition will lead to the persecution of God's people (Rev 6:9-11).

The Terrible Beast

As the Time of Distress progresses, the true character of this political power will be revealed and people will realise that it opposes God. Many Christians will wake up and realise that the mighty empire that they trust has morphed into the Terrible Beast of Revelation and Daniel.

> The king will do as he pleases... He will be successful until the time of wrath is completed, for what has been determined must take place (Dan 11:36).

Many Christians will miss the emergence of the Beast, because they are looking for a wicked man, who gains control by devious means and then wreaks evil on the world. This is a mistake. The Terrible Beast is not a manifestation of evil and wickedness, as many assume. This view has been spread by movies and books, but it distorts the truth (keyword: Terrible Beast).

Role of the Beast

The book of Revelation explains that the Beast will do four things. They are not what most Christians are expecting.

1. Blasphemy

> The beast was given a mouth to utter proud words and blasphemies.... It opened its mouth to blaspheme God, and to slander his name and his dwelling place and those who live in heaven (Rev 13:5-6).

A person blaspheming usually speaks against God to mock him, but the Beast speaks "proud words," not rude words. It insults God by claiming his place and offering a salvation that is better than the salvation bought by Jesus.

> He will speak against the Most High and...try to change the set times and the laws (Dan 7:25).

Political messiahs promise to provide human salvation using political power. Most people believe there is no God, so a human government is their only hope. The Beast is an attempt to create a better world by applying human wisdom to government. It is not established by evil men to do evil, but is instituted by good men to do good.

2. Economic Control

The Beast will control the economic system to prevent economic collapse.

> It also forced all people, great and small, rich and poor, free and slave (Rev 13:16).

Political powers have always manipulated the little people and the poor. Their misery does not change, but this Beast will also control the rich and the powerful. It even controls those who are too big to fail (the great and the free). These activities will make preferred merchants and traders very rich (Rev 18:11-20).

3. Worldwide Influence

Authority and influence will be surrendered to this dominant nation by governments all over the world (Rev 13:5).

58

> And it was given authority over every tribe, people,
> language and nation (Rev 13:7).

> For God has put it into their hearts to fulfil His purpose,
> to be of one mind, and to give their kingdom to the beast,
> until the words of God are fulfilled (Rev 17:17).

The nations do not disappear during this period. They carry on, but give some of their sovereignty to this dominant nation, so it can deal with the crises sweeping the earth.

John calls this behaviour adultery.

> The kings of the earth committed adultery with her, and
> the merchants of the earth grew rich from her excessive
> luxuries (Rev 18:3).

The nations belong to God, so they should be loyal to him. Instead, they surrender to a powerful nation for comfort and prosperity. They compromise to get what they want.

Daniel indicates that some nations will be broken up by the Beast (Dan 7:7). This has already happened in Yugoslavia, Somalia and Sudan. In the future, many nations will be split up by the Beast.

4. Christians Persecuted

Christians who do not accept the authority and the power of the Beast will face terrible persecution.

> It was given power to wage war against God's holy people
> and to conquer them (Rev 13:7).

> If anyone is to go into captivity, into captivity they will go.
> If anyone is to be killed with the sword, with the sword
> they will be killed (Rev 13:10).

Some Christians will understand that the Beast is a false messiah offering a false hope and warn of the dangers of trusting this dominant nation.

> This calls for patient endurance and faithfulness on the
> part of God's people (Rev 13:10).

The main role of the Beast is to persecute Christians to create a suffering church that is ready to receive the Kingdom.

This powerful nation does not engage in blatant evil. It controls trade and puts big business back in its place. It promises to bring peace and prosperity to the people of the world. These are things that all good governments are expected to do. Many Christians are already applauding this nation for its exercise of power throughout the world.

Israel

Daniel prophesied that multitudes from his nation would receive salvation after a Time of Distress.

> There will be a **time of distress** such as has not happened from the beginning of nations until then. But at that time your people—everyone whose name is found written in the book—will be delivered (Dan 12:1).

Before this promise can be fulfilled, Daniel's people will endure a season of distress. This time of trouble comes because, Jewish leaders have rushed ahead of God and used political manipulation and military power to establish their own nation state before the Times of the Gentiles have ended. Ezekiel speaks of people who have returned to the land by the power of the sword.

> A land that is restored by the sword, whose inhabitants have been gathered from many nations to the mountains of Israel who had long been desolate.... and now all of them live in safety (Ez 38:8).

The Jewish people responded to the trauma of their holocaust in Europe, by seeking security in a Jewish state. This will prove to be a false hope, because during the Times of the Gentiles, their security comes from being scattered among the nations.

> The woman was given the two wings of a great eagle, so that she might fly to the place prepared for her in the wilderness, where she would be taken care of for a **time, times and half a time**, out of the serpent's reach (Rev 12:14).

God has fulfilled this promise by keeping the Jewish people alive among the nations for two thousand years. When they gather in one place, they lose this protection. Trusting in political and military power leaves them vulnerable to the powers of evil. The Jewish people will only be safe in their land, when they trust in God through Jesus.

No Protection

Jesus had warned Israel that their house would be desolate until they blessed those coming in his name (Matt 23:39). He had previously warned how damaging this could be.

> When an impure spirit comes out of a person, it goes through arid places seeking rest and does not find it. Then it says, 'I will return to the house I left.' When it arrives, it finds the house unoccupied, swept clean and put in order. Then it goes and takes with it seven other spirits more wicked than itself, and they go in and live there. And the final condition of that person is worse than the first. That is how it will be with this wicked generation (Matt 12:43-45).

This was a warning for an entire generation. The current generation in Israel has amassed a huge arsenal of conventional and nuclear weapons, yet it has a no spiritual protection. Without the cross and the Spirit, they have no way of dealing with evil spirits.

This chink in Israel's armour has allowed a huge host of evil spirits to flood this small nation, carried by people who do not understand what is happening. Jewish migrants from Russia often bring spirits of violence and control with them. When Israeli children visit Auschwitz, the emotions produced by the memory of the Holocaust open them up to spirits of violence and hatred that are wandering around there looking for a home. These children often take these spirits home without realising what is happening. Bringing these spirits together allows them to form hierarchies that leverage their power. The house of Israel is now the home of thousands of spirits of fear, hatred, pride, deception, anger and violence. They are currently biding their time, with the deceiving spirits covering for their more violent colleagues.

Rash Action

During the Time of Distress, a host of evil spirits will break out and cause the political leadership of Israel to go ugly. Violent and angry leaders will take rash actions in an attempt to force things to happen.

> Sons of the destroyers among your own people will rebel in fulfilment of the vision, but without success (Dan 11:14).

While the nations are distracted by other disturbances in the Middle East, violent people will use force to push their agenda for the Jewish dominance of greater Israel. Their strategy will fail and bring the wrath of the nations down on Israel. This disaster will end with Israel being invaded. An army led by a powerful western nation will overrun the nation of Israel from bases in the Middle East.

> The invader will do as he pleases; no one will be able to stand against him. He will establish himself in the Beautiful Land and will have the power to destroy it (Dan 11:16).

The expression "power to destroy" is literally "destruction in his hand". The invading army will have weapons of mass destruction, making resistance impossible.

> And he shall set his face to come with the strength of his whole kingdom, and with him equitable conditions; and he shall perform them (Dan 11:17).

This powerful western nation will take control of Israel in an attempt to impose a lasting peace in the Middle East. Its President will use military power to force Israel into a more equitable solution to the Palestinian problem. Israel might be forced to accept an independent Palestinian state. Ironically, Israel will get the security it seeks from independence while being trampled by a powerful nation.

The nations that invade Israel will come under the influence of the evil spirits that have gathered there. Their leaders will come under the same spirits of hatred, pride, violence and destruction. They will go on to do great evil throughout the world.

Israel Humbled

In subsequent decades, several external rulers will gain control of Israel. The nation will continue to be trampled by the Gentiles as Jesus had warned (Luke 21:24). Jews who have come to Israel seeking peace will be disappointed.

John warned that the Jewish people would be in exile for a time, times and half a time (Rev 12:14). When Daniel asked an angel how long the manoeuvrings of powerful nations would last, he received the same answer, with a warning.

> The man clothed in linen, who was above the waters of the river, lifted his right hand and his left hand toward heaven, and I heard him swear by him who lives forever, saying, "It will be for a *time, times and half a time*. When the power of the holy people has been *finally broken*, all these things will be completed" (Dan 12:7).

The "holy people" is Israel. The angel declares that the power of Israel will be broken after a "time, times and half a time", which is the end of the Times of the Gentiles.

The Zionist movement used the manoeuvrings of powerful nations to achieve a return to their land. This has placed the Jewish people at enormous risk. The Israeli government has mitigated this risk by accumulating massive military force, and the Israeli people now trust this for their security. This false trust will have to be broken before the people of Israel are able to believe in Jesus. Military defeat will break Israeli faith in their political leaders and military power, opening the way for faith in Jesus.

When several nations are attacking Israel and there is great trauma in the land, the Holy Spirit will be poured out.

> There will be a *time of distress* such as has not happened from the beginning of nations until then. But at that time your people—everyone whose name is found written in the book—will be delivered. (Dan 12:1).

The trauma that climaxes the Time of Distress leads to the Fullness of the Jews (keyword: Israel).

The Church

The Time of Distress will be a huge disappointment for many Christians, especially those who trust false teachings.

- People who trust the prosperity gospel will find themselves suffering.
- Christians hoping for a rapture rescue will find themselves living through tribulation (keyword: Rescue).
- Christians who see the state of Israel as proof of God's faithfulness will be disillusioned when Israel is invaded by a western nation (not Iran or Russia).
- People who believe in democracy will be shattered when their governments begin to persecute them.
- Christians who trust the protection of the state will be shocked when it collapses.

Most Christians will be unprepared for the Time of Distress. Many will be thrown into confusion and despair. Some will fall from the faith (keyword: Tribulation).

Suffering

During the Time of Distress, the church will suffer for Jesus. The letter to the Hebrews describes what it will be like.

> You stood your ground in the face of suffering. Sometimes you were publicly exposed to insult and persecution; at other times you stood side by side with those who were so treated. You joyfully accepted the confiscation of your property (Heb 10:32-34).

This season will be tough for those who follow Jesus. They will have to turn the other cheek again and again.

- Many will be ripped off by violent and ruthless men.
- People will be killed for the food they have stored.
- Human life will be cheap.
- The protection of the state will disappear.
- Justice will be rare.
- Suffering will lead to victory.

Prepare

Looking for the second coming or rapture during the Time of Distress will lead to disappointment. Instead of trying to escape, Christians should:

- understand that the powers of evil will not give up without a fight;
- prepare for persecution;
- build strong communities where Christians will be safe;
- raise up a prophetic voice that understands the times;
- speak prophetically to the nations;
- pray for the real salvation of Israel, not military victory;
- speak prophetically to the people of Israel to prepare them for faith in Jesus.

During a time of trouble, the safest place is a strong Christian community. Paul insists that we counter evil with good.

> Do not be overcome by evil, but overcome evil with good (Rom 12:21).

In the same letter, he gives instructions about building strong relationships with other Christians.

> Be devoted to one another in brotherly love.
> Honor one another above yourselves.
> Share with God's people who are in need.
> Practice hospitality.
> Live in harmony with one another (Rom 12:10,13,16).

The best antidote to evil is strong communities where Christians can stand together to protect those coming under attack. Those standing alone will be vulnerable. Faithful prayer during affliction produces joyful hope.

> Be joyful in hope,
> patient in affliction,
> faithful in prayer (Rom 12:12).

Not the Tribulation

This Time of Distress and trouble will be a time of persecution for Christians. As the world slips into turmoil, political power will be consolidated in a desperate attempt to hold back the chaos. One mighty nation will gain influence over a large part of the earth by promising to restore peace and prosperity. Christians will see through the promises and stand against them. This Beast will use its power to annihilate any opposition, which will be very painful for many believers. However, because it opposes God, the situation will deteriorate even more.

God will allow this persecution to purify the church and make it ready to receive the Kingdom. Christians who are not fully devoted to the Lord will fall away, but those who stay true will be strengthened by the refining process.

> To the one who is victorious and does my will to the end,
> I will give authority over the nations (Rev 2:26).

Christians who suffer for Jesus will inherit his Kingdom.

This Time of Distress should not be called "The Tribulation". Many Christians will experience terrible trials, but this will be no different from the experience of Christians down through the ages. Describing this time as something unique is unfair to Christians in other times who have suffered terribly for the Lord.

Being under pressure is normal for Christians. We are taught that we should always expect tribulation.

> In the world you have tribulation, but take courage,
> I have overcome the world (John 16:33).

> We must go through many tribulations to enter the kingdom of God (Acts 14:22).

Christians should always expect tribulation. Whenever they are true to Christ, they will be a threat to the world, and this will always bring opposition. The Time of Distress will be very painful, but Christians will take comfort from knowing that God will cut this terrible season short. They will rejoice in these trials, as they will see the Kingdom of God springing forth on earth.

▶ Big Battle

The epochal event that marks the end of the Time of Distress is a Big Battle.

When the Time of Distress is getting rough, the remaining political powers will engage in a battle to the death.

- The battle will emerge out of a series of skirmishes between the Western Beast and the Islamic powers.
- Trade wars will break out in various places.
- Control of oil fields will be a big issue.
- Minor military powers will seize local trade routes.
- China will take advantage of the situation and push into Central Asia to secure control of minerals and oil.
- The Western Beast will be used to getting its own way. It will enter various confrontations, assuming that old enemies will be intimidated and back down, as in the past. This time these enemies will push back.
- The Eastern powers will get tired of being pushed around by the Western Beast and will decide to have a go too (Rev 16:12-14).
- The Islamic nations will attack Israel to plunder and loot the precious metals that were stored there during earlier economic crises (Ez 38:12-13).
- These nations will want to punish the Beast for its policies while controlling the promised land. They will believe it has not gone far enough, so they will attack it where it is exposed in Israel (Dan 11:40-45).
- The major players in the Big Battle will be the Beast, representing the West, the Islamic nations inspired by the Prince of Persia, and the powers from the East. Russia is too weak to be more than a bit player.

The Old Testament prophets focus on the combat in Israel, because that was their interest, but the battle will take place on a much broader scale (Rev 16:19).

Different Battle

The Big Battle will become a personal struggle between
political leaders. For most of history, war was a struggle
between one king and another, with each being supported by
a small retinue of followers. Ordinary people did not get
involved, unless they lived close to the battlefield. The
nature of warfare changed dramatically with the emergence
of nationalism. War stopped being a contest between kings
and became a struggle between nations. Nations tend to
fight over causes, and everyone is drawn into the struggle.

During the Time of Distress, war between nations will
transform into personal struggles between political leaders
(Dan 11). Assassinations of political leaders will be used to
project the Beast's power. Fear of death will cause many to
submit to the Beast. The weapons of war will change.

- Large concentrations of infantry will be superfluous.
- Independent mobile strike teams will be efficient tools
  for strategic assassinations.
- Predator drones will intimidate people by keeping them
  under surveillance and threat of attack. They will only
  kill a few people, but will torment many (Rev 9:1-6).
- Mobile missile launchers will kill more (Rev 9:17-19).
- Remote-controlled weapons will project power across
  great distance.

Caught in the Middle

The global struggle between the big powers will spill over
into Israel. This is often called the battle of Armageddon,
but that is a misunderstanding of a single verse in Revelation.

> Then they gathered the kings together to the place that in
> Hebrew is called Armageddon (Rev 16:16).

John was not describing the site of the Big Battle, but
explaining how it affects Israel. The Hebrew words trans-
literated as Armageddon refer to the Mount of Megiddo,

which is seared in Jewish memories as the place where King Josiah died. He was one of Judah's best kings. At the peak of his career, he was drawn into in a battle between Egypt and Assyria and killed by a random arrow. Jeremiah composed a lament, because his death was a tragic waste and Judah never had a good king again (2 Chron 35:20-25).

The Big Battle will be the same. Israel will be drawn into the posturing between the Western Beast and the Islamic powers in the same way that Josiah got caught between Egypt and Assyria (Ezek 38,39; Dan 11:40-45).

Joel says that the nations will be gathered in the Valley of Jehoshaphat (Joel 3:12). This is not a place, but an explanation. The word Jehoshaphat means "God judges". This event will bring judgement on the powerful nations.

Christian Prophets

At the peak of the Big Battle, God will intervene decisively.

> The Lord will lay bare his holy arm in the sight of all the nations, and all the ends of the earth will see the salvation of our God (Is 52:10).

When Israel is besieged and the people are full of fear, Christian prophets will speak out and warn the nations gathered for battle that they will be destroyed. These prophets will speak protective judgment in Jesus name. Their prayers will release God's hand (Is 62:6-7).

The Christian prophets will encourage the Jewish people to trust in God. They will warn that trust in military power will disappoint. This message was foreshadowed by Isaiah.

> Comfort, comfort my people, says your God. Speak tenderly to Jerusalem, and proclaim to her that her hard service has been completed, that her sin has been paid for, that she has received from the Lord's hand double for all her sins (Is 40:1-2).

Prophets will announce that Israel's spiritual exile has ended. They will promise that Israel will be delivered by the power of the Holy Spirit, and not by military force (Zeph 3:14-16). The people of Israel will not believe them, but when deliverance comes, they will remember their words and will bless those who prophesied in Jesus name. This is the true sign that the Times of the Gentiles has ended.

> Look, your house is left to you desolate... until you say, 'Blessed is he who comes in the name of the Lord' (Matt 23:38-39).

These prophets must be scrupulous about timing. Announcing Israel's return to blessing before God gives the word would undermine their authority. Many Christian prophets have already disqualified themselves for this role by announcing the end of Israel's desolation before God has spoken. These prophets will have no credibility if they were required to promise deliverance for Israel during a time of great disaster, because they have promised this before and been proved wrong.

The prayers and declarations of the Christian prophets will release the power of the Holy Spirit. He will bring about the destruction of the political and military powers of the world in several different ways.

- Atmospheric conditions will cause remote-controlled weapons to go haywire.
- Computer viruses and worms will sabotage the control of weapons.
- Some of the people controlling the weapons will fall into confusion and turn their weapons on themselves.

> Every man's sword will be against his brother (Ezek 38:21).
>
> On that day people will be stricken by the Lord with great panic. They will seize each other by the hand and attack one another (Zech 14:13).

The outcome will be amazing.

- The military forces invading Israel will totally destroy themselves. Their destruction is described in Zechariah 14:12-14 and Ezekiel 39:3-5.

70

- Destruction will backfire on the nations these armies come from. Their political leaders will be destroyed.
    The cities of the nations collapsed (Rev 16:19).

The declarations of the prophets will deliver Israel.

Suffering Prophets

John saw these Christian prophets being called (Rev 10:9-10).
    Take it and eat it. It will turn your stomach sour, but in
    your mouth it will be as sweet as honey (Rev 10:9).

When these prophets are called to their ministry, it will seem to be a sweet calling. Once they begin to fulfil their calling, they will suffer for their faith and it will suddenly feel quite sour. The prophets will lead the way for the suffering church by passing through suffering first. When they have suffered for Jesus, they will be ready to prophesy to the nations and release God's purposes on earth.

    Then I was told, "You must prophesy again about many
    peoples, nations, languages and kings" (Rev 10:11).

The suffering prophets will release the events that end the Time of Distress and open the way for the Kingdom of God (keyword: Prophetic Ministry).

Epochal Non Event

A key epochal event does not occur at the end the Time of Distress. Jesus does not return at the end of season to deliver Israel, as many Christians expect.

- Christians hoping to be rescued by the second coming will be disappointed.
- The Time of Distress brings the end of the Times of the Gentiles, not the end of history.
- Jesus returns at the end of history to wind up life on earth. He does not return to Jerusalem to reign over a Jewish empire called the Kingdom of God.
- The next season is the Kingdom of God, which is the work of the Holy Spirit.

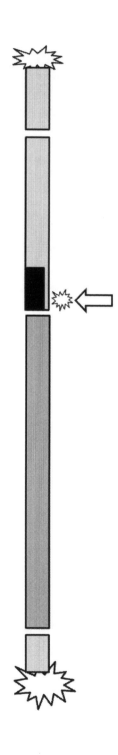

7

Fullness of Israel

The Big Battle is the epochal event that ends the Time of Distress. Three epochal events mark the beginning of the next season. They open the way for the Holy Spirit to be released to bring transformation of the earth.

- The Fullness of Israel;
- Collapse of Human Governments;
- The Advance of the Gospel.

Fullness of Israel

The Fullness of Israel marks the beginning of a new season. Traditionally, this event has been called the "calling of the Jews", but "fullness" is the biblical term.

> Now if their fall is riches for the world, and their failure riches for the Gentiles, how much more their *fullness* (Rom.11:12)!

This epochal event is the major turning point in history.

Looking at the history of the Jewish people, it would be easy to believe that God is finished with them. That is not true. Although they are under God's judgment for rejecting their Messiah, the Bible promises they will be restored to a place of blessing. This will happen when they acknowledge that Jesus is the Messiah they have been seeking.

This diagram illustrates God's covenant with Israel.

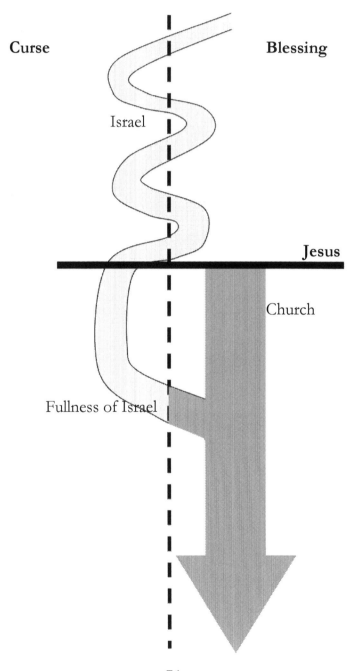

To the left of the dotted line is the curse of the covenant. On the right of the dotted line is covenant blessing. The pale grey represents the history of Israel. The ministry of Jesus is represented by the black line. Israel rejected Jesus and passed to the left under the curse of the law (Matthew 23:37-39). Jesus fulfilled the terms of the covenant on behalf of all those who believe in him, so the church (dark grey) lives in the blessing of the covenant. As the church grows, the grey arrow will become much larger.

Israel is currently on the left of the dotted line, under the curse. The nation of Israel was established "by the sword" (Ezekiel 38:8) and not the direct hand of God, so it will continue being trampled by the Gentiles. However, God has not forgotten his covenant, so at the right time, he will restore Israel back onto the side of blessing.

The Promise

God's promise to Israel is most clearly stated in Romans 11. The Jews have stumbled, but did not fall beyond recovery (Rom 11:11). Israel will eventually be reconciled to the Lord. Although the Jews became enemies of God by rejecting the gospel, their election is sure for the sake of the patriarchs.

> As far as the gospel is concerned, they are enemies for your sake; but as far as election is concerned, they are loved on account of the patriarchs, for God's gifts and his call are irrevocable (Rom 11:28-29).

Once God calls a people he does not change that calling (Is 54:10, Jer 31:37).

When the Fullness of Israel comes, the vast majority of Jews will believe in Jesus. Paul described this as being grafted back into the olive tree.

> If they do not persist in unbelief, they will be grafted in, for God is able to graft them in again (Rom 11:23).

They have been shut out for a time, but will be restored to blessing when the Times of the Gentiles are complete.

> Israel has experienced a hardening in part until the
> **fullness of the Gentiles** has come in, and in this way all
> Israel will be saved (Rom 11:25-26).

The church and Israel will become one in Jesus.

Salvation will come to most Jews at the same time. When their entire nation is touched by the Spirit in a time of trouble, large numbers will come to faith together. This restoration is based on a promise in the book of Moses.

> But if from there you seek the Lord your God, you will
> find him if you seek him with all your heart and with all
> your soul. When you are in **distress** and all these things
> have happened to you, then in later days you will return to
> the Lord your God and obey him (Deut 4:29-30).

When Israel was dispersed among the nations, God was not breaking his covenant. The exile was the fulfilment of the curses specified in the covenant, so when that punishment is complete, Israel can receive the blessings of the covenant again (see Isaiah 51:17-23).

How

Many Christians are confused about how the Fullness of Israel occurs. God's solution always fits the problem. The Jewish problem is "seeing". Their eyes have been blinded to prevent them from seeing the truth.

> God gave them a spirit of stupor, eyes that could not see
> and ears that could not hear, to this very day. (Rom 11:8).

> Israel has experienced a hardening in part until the fullness
> of the Gentiles has come in (Rom 11:25).

This spiritual blindness lasts until the end of the Times of the Gentiles. The Jews need to have their spiritual eyes opened and their hearts cracked before they can receive salvation (this is the only way anyone can come to salvation).

Zechariah prophesied that when the nations besieging Israel are destroyed in response to prophetic prayer, God will pour his spirit out on Israel and open their eyes to understand that Jesus is their messiah.

> I will pour out on the house of David and the inhabitants of Jerusalem a spirit of grace and supplication. They will look on me, the one they have pierced, and they will mourn for him as one mourns for an only child, and grieve bitterly for him as one grieves for a firstborn son (Zech 12:10).

At the end of Times of the Gentiles, the Spirit of the Lord will be poured into the hearts of Israel. They will receive the Spirit and cry out to Jesus for salvation. The Holy Spirit of grace will give them faith to believe in him.

The Holy Spirit will open the eyes of their hearts. They will stop looking for a warlike messiah and realise that Jesus "who was pieced" by a spear is their messiah. This realisation will produce a great flood of repentance. As Israel realises that Jesus reigns at the right hand of God and that they have been saved by the prayers in his name, the whole land will be filled with tears. When they realise what Jesus has done for them, they will weep with sadness and joy. The weeping will be greater than when King Josiah died (Zech 12:11-14).

Many Christians believe that the Jews will be converted when Jesus returns to Jerusalem, but this could not work. Seeing is not believing. The Jews saw Jesus for three years while he was on earth, but they did not believe in him, because their hearts were hard (Rom 10). Nothing has changed, so seeing Jesus again would not bring them to faith. Israel's problem is hardness of heart and the only cure for spiritual blindness is the revelation of the Holy Spirit.

The Jewish people will not come to salvation by seeing Jesus return to Jerusalem. Their hearts will be changed when the Holy Spirit moves to open their spiritual eyes.

> I will no longer hide my face from them, for I will pour out my Spirit on the people of Israel, declares the Sovereign Lord (Ezek 39:29).

> I will pour out my Spirit on your offspring, and my blessing on your descendants (Is 44:3).

The Jews will be converted by an outpouring of the Spirit and the preaching of a prophetic church. This is not a change in game plan. The Jews receive salvation like everyone else, by repenting and believing in Jesus.

Blessing to the World

The fullness of the Jews will usher in a time of great blessing for the world.

> But if their transgression means riches for the world, and their loss means riches for the Gentiles, how much greater riches will their full inclusion bring (Rom 11:12)!

This happens in two ways:

1. When Jewish desolation comes to an end, Satan's legal authority on earth will be gone, so he will be easily routed. As Christians bind his authority, he will be exposed as weak and feeble. With evil massively curtailed, the biggest obstacle to the Kingdom will be gone. A rapid decline in evil will open the way for the Kingdom of God.

2. The Fullness of the Jews is not just blessing for Israel, it means "life from the dead" for the church.

   > For if their rejection brought reconciliation to the world, what will their acceptance be but life from the dead (Rom 11:12).

   The Jews will be back in the team where they belong. The church will no longer be truncated. The Holy Spirit will no longer be constrained by part of the body of Jesus being missing. With his team complete, the Holy Spirit will have a new freedom to work in the world

The Fullness of the Jews opens the way for a rapid advance of the gospel. God will be free to pour out his Spirit and bring his Kingdom to fulfilment.

This event is the major turning point in history, so Christians should be working and praying for this time to come. They should be praying for the Jews to be restored to a place of blessing, so blessing will return to the entire world. (Prayer for the military success of Israel will not do it.)

Revelation

John received several visions of the fullness of the Jews.

> Then I heard the number of those who were sealed:
> 144,000 from all the tribes of Israel (Rev 7:4).

The numbers sealed are symbolic not literal. Ten symbolises completeness and twelve represents Israel. 12 squared times 10 cubed is a perfect symbol for the fullness of Israel. Twelve is also the number representing the apostles. This is a promise that Israel will fulfil the apostolic calling announced to Abraham (Gen 12:3) and Moses (Deut 4:6-7).

> Then I looked, and there before me was the Lamb, standing on Mount Zion, and with him 144,000 who had his name and his Father's name written on their foreheads. And I heard a sound from heaven like the roar of rushing waters and like a loud peal of thunder. The sound I heard was like that of harpists playing their harps. And they sang a new song before the throne and before the four living creatures and the elders. No one could learn the song except the 144,000 who had been redeemed from the earth... They were purchased from among mankind and offered as firstfruits to God and the Lamb (Rev 14:1-4).

This is the fulfilment of the sealing seen in an earlier vision. It leads to a powerful advance of the gospel.

> Then I saw another angel flying in midair, and he had the eternal gospel to proclaim to those who live on the earth—to every nation, tribe, language and people (Rev 14:6).

The eternal gospel will be proclaimed to all those who live on earth.

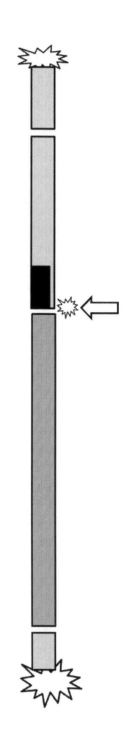

8

Collapse of Governments

The Time of Distress ends when human governments collapse under the weight of their failed programs and broken promises. If their rise to power is grand, their collapse will be spectacular. Faith in human government and political power will be destroyed forever.

Human political power is a huge obstacle to the Kingdom, because it undermines God's authority and offers a false salvation. The spread of democracy has increased this faith. Before the Holy Spirit can bring the Kingdom of God to fullness, this widespread trust in human political power must be swept away.

For most of human history, the world has been controlled by kings, emperors and sundry political powers. During the last few centuries, various democratic demagogues have taken this controlling role. Before the Kingdom of God can come to fullness on earth, this human political power must be destroyed. The Christian prophets who comfort Israel will also announce the destruction of political power. Their prophetic words will release the power of the Holy Spirit to bring down human government and political empires throughout the world.

Governments Collapse

The opening of the sixth seal describes the collapse of human government and democratic power.

> I watched as he opened the sixth seal. There was a great earthquake. The sun turned black like sackcloth made of goat hair, the whole moon turned blood red, and the stars in the sky fell to earth, as late figs drop from a fig tree when shaken by a strong wind. The sky receded like a scroll, rolling up, and every mountain and island was removed from its place (Rev 6:12-14).

These events are not literal. The Old Testament prophets often described the collapse of a great nation in the same language. Ezekiel's prophecy about Egypt is an example.

> When I snuff you out, I will cover the heavens and darken their stars; I will cover the sun with a cloud, and the moon will not give its light (Ez 32:7).

This is a description of the collapse of Egypt at the hand of Babylon. The sun continued to shine, but the prophecy was fulfilled. Other prophets used the sun, moon and stars turning to blood or falling from the sky to describe the collapse of human government and political power.

Politicians Flee

The disastrous end to the Time of Distress will destroy the confidence of political leaders throughout the entire world.

> Then the kings of the earth and the great men and the commanders and the rich and the strong and every slave and free man hid themselves in the caves and among the rocks of the mountains; and they said to the mountains and to the rocks, "Fall on us and hide us from the presence of Him who sits on the throne, and from the wrath of the Lamb" (Rev 6:15-16).

The stars falling from the sky are kings and rulers losing their power. Instead of strutting on the world stage, politicians and kings will hide under the rocks and caves. Those who have trusted in political power will be filled with terror.

- Political leaders will flee their offices.

- No one will be willing to take their place.
- The money will be gone and stresses will be huge, so no one will want political power.
- The existing political order will collapse in all nations.

As the empire of man is nearing its last gasp, human governments will collapse and disappear everywhere. When the people of the world see the harm done by their leaders' policies, they will be furious. The leaders who are not destroyed by war will be hounded out of office by violent mobs. They will try to escape, but will find no place to hide.

People who trust their government to provide security and prosperity will be shocked when nothing happens. Those who call on their political leaders to make decisions about the future will find that there is no one there. That will be scary for many people, but they will not be as scared as the politicians themselves.

Best Government Ever Fails

The Time of Distress will climax in a great rush of pride that attempts to create a perfect government and spread its influence throughout the world. Hopes will be high, because this government will be formed by good people with strong Christian support. However, excess political power always leads to disaster. The Democratic Beast that has promised peace for the world will be overrun by chaos and collapse in a terrible mess.

People are not surprised when evil leaders do harm, but they expect democratic government to be a force for good. When this good democratic political power collapses in a morass of troubles, those who have relied on it will be totally disillusioned. The collapse of the best human government ever will be so horrifying that the people of the world will never trust human political power again.

- Confidence in political power will be shaken.

- Human government will be exposed as a false hope.

- Faith in democracy will be crushed.

- Trust in military force will be smashed.

- Confidence in police and security forces will be broken.

- The principalities and power will be totally disarmed.

- Political power will crumble, collapse and sneak away.

The faith in political power that hides in human hearts will vanish forever.

Principalities and Power

Political power and spiritual warfare are linked. The leaders of a nation or city have authority over the citizens of their domain. This creates an opportunity for the powers of evil to attack people with political power to gain influence over those under their authority. Once the powers of evil gain control over a political leader, people under the leader's authority are vulnerable to the same attack.

Concentrating on political powers enables the forces of evil to expand their power. If an evil spirit gains control over one person, it can make that person's life miserable. If the same spirit gets control over a king or president, it can control a nation. Most of the power of evil is an illusion. By concentrating their attacks on a few powerful people, the forces of evil have leveraged their limited power. Political power has amplified the power of spiritual evil.

If the forces of evil attach themselves to a king or president, they become "principalities and powers" with power over everyone in the nation. When we submit to political leaders, we open our lives to the spiritual forces controlling them. Concentration of political power shifts spiritual power to the principalities and powers.

When human rulers and empires fall, the principalities and powers that have amplified their power through them will be shattered. With no place to stand, they will just be common evil spirits defeated by the cross. When political leaders lose their power, the spiritual forces that have dominated the world through them will be powerless too. They will be diffused through society and become fragmented and weak.

The Kingdom Emerges

The democratic empire that accumulates vast political powers in a vain attempt to bring peace will collapse into such a mess that the people of the world will not trust human political power again. Christians do not need to fight against this human political empire, because God will come in judgment against it. He will annihilate the ultimate human government, killing the credibility of political power forever.

> But the court will sit for judgment, and his dominion will be taken away, annihilated and destroyed forever (Dan 7:26).

When human governments stop functioning, a power vacuum will exist. Those who have trusted in democratic government will be desperate for something different and better. With the ultimate human government crushed by events it could not control, people will be desperate for a saviour who keeps his promises. The Kingdom of God will appear very attractive to them.

Political power will be chopped up, pushed down and spread around to ordinary people who trust and obey Jesus and walk in the Spirit. The kingdoms of the world will disappear and be replaced by the Kingdom of God.

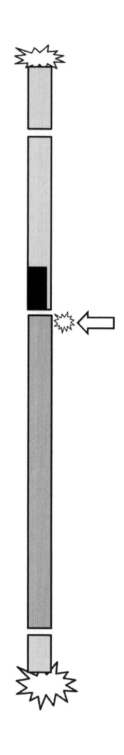

9

Advance of the Gospel

The collapse of human government and the fullness of Israel are the epochal events that mark the end of the Time of Distress. These events release the Holy Spirit to carry the gospel to the world. The Advance of the Gospel marks the beginning of the next season. Several changes make a rapid advance of the gospel possible.

- With all constraints gone, the Holy Spirit will be free to do his stuff in a new way.
- The suffering of the Time of Distress will have purified the church. It will be radical and ready to proclaim the good news.
- The gospel will be preached in the power of the Spirit. He will accompany the gospel with signs and wonders that confirm the love and power of God (Mark 16:16-17).
- Christians will have been forced to build strong relationships with each other in order to survive through the Time of Distress. People will be able to see the new commandment being lived out in their neighbourhoods (John 13:34). They will be drawn to Christians loving each other as Jesus loves them.

- People who have experienced Christian generosity during tough times will have tested this love and proved it is real.
- Jewish Christians will preach the gospel of the Kingdom with zeal and fervour throughout the world.
- The nations of the world will have trusted human government for peace and prosperity. When peace and prosperity are stripped away, and governments go down the gurgler, people will be desperate for a better saviour. Jesus will stand out from the pack.
- The principalities and powers will be crippled by the collapse of human governments.

The Eternal Gospel

After the sealing of Israel (Rev 7:1-8), John saw great multitudes being saved by the gospel.

> After this I looked, and there before me was a great multitude that no one could count, from every nation, tribe, people and language, standing before the throne and before the Lamb. They were wearing white robes (Rev 7:9-10).

The number of people saved by the gospel will be a multitude so large that no one can count them. When the Times of the Gentiles are complete and the Jews join the team, this promise will be fulfilled.

A vision of the 144,000, representing the Fullness of Israel (Rev 14:1-4), is followed by the gospel going to the nations.

> Then I saw another angel flying in midair, and he had the eternal gospel to proclaim to those who live on the earth— to every nation, tribe, language and people (Rev 14:6).

When Israel has received the gospel, the church that includes Israel will proclaim the gospel of Jesus to the entire world.

Harvest of the Earth

The proclamation of the gospel leads to the great harvest of the earth. John saw Jesus sitting on a cloud with a sickle in his hand. An angel is given a sickle to harvest the earth.

> Then another angel came out of the temple and called in a
> loud voice to him who was sitting on the cloud, "Take
> your sickle and reap, because the time to reap has come,
> for the harvest of the earth is ripe." So he who was seated
> on the cloud swung his sickle over the earth, and the earth
> was harvested (Rev 14:15-16).

When the Time of Distress is complete, the harvest on earth will be ripe. Jesus will send out his gospel messengers to bring in his harvest. The great harvest comes after the Fullness of the Jews and it brings in the Kingdom of God.

After his vision of the earth being harvested, John saw those who had been victorious in suffering standing on a sea of glass and praising God. They were singing the song of Moses and the Lamb.

> Great and marvelous are your deeds, Lord God Almighty.
> Just and true are your ways, King of the nations. Who will
> not fear you, Lord, and bring glory to your name? For you
> alone are holy. All nations will come and worship before
> you, for your righteous acts have been revealed (Rev 15:3-4).

These words come to fulfilment when the covenant of Moses and the gospel of Jesus are brought together in unity by the Spirit of God. When the nations see the glory of God's Kingdom, they will all surrender and worship God.

> For the earth will be filled with the knowledge of the glory
> of the Lord, as the waters cover the sea (Hab 2:14).

Power of the Gospel

The effectiveness of the gospel will be seen in the land of Israel. The gospel of Jesus and the gift of the Holy Spirit will change the hearts of the Israelis and the Palestinians allowing them to live together in unity. They will tear down the dividing wall that has been built as a barrier between them.

> He has destroyed the barrier, the dividing wall of hostility
> (Eph 2:14-16).

The destruction of this wall will amaze the watching world and demonstrate the power of the gospel.

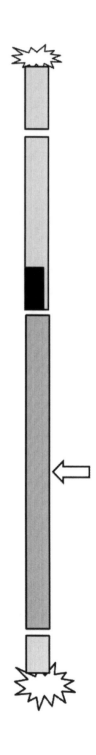

10

Kingdom of God

Best Season Ever

The Advance of the Gospel opens the way for the Kingdom of God. During this season, God's will is done on earth as it is done in heaven. This is the best season in human history. The Kingdom of God, that Jesus proclaimed was near, will come to fulfilment and bring great blessing on earth.

The time will be right for the coming of the Kingdom. All obstacles will be gone and the ingredients prepared.

- Suffering for Jesus will have prepared the church.

- The church will finally lose interest in domination and control and will be committed to love and service.

- Christians will be ready to receive the Kingdom without being corrupted by power.

- The Fullness of Israel will give the Holy Spirit freedom to work through the church to transform the world.

- All forms of human government will have been tried and failed. People will be desperate for something better.

- The people of the world will hate being governed by

man, so they will be open to the government of God.

- The spiritual forces of evil will be defused by the downfall of human power.

- As human political powers are swept away, authority will return to families and local communities.

Daniel's vision climaxes when the people of God receive the Kingdom.

> The holy people of the Most High will receive the kingdom and will possess it forever—yes, for ever and ever (Dan 7:18).

This is not the second coming, because Jesus is seated in the presence of God throughout the vision.

> He approached the Ancient of Days and was led into his presence (Dan 7:13).

Jesus received glory and authority at the ascension.

> He was given authority, glory and sovereign power; all nations and peoples of every language worshiped him. His dominion is an everlasting dominion that will not pass away, and his kingdom is one that will never be destroyed (Dan 7:14).

He does not need to return to earth to establish his Kingdom. It comes to fullness on earth when his people receive the authority that he has in heaven.

> Then the kingdom and dominion, and the greatness of the kingdoms under the whole heaven, shall be given to the people, the saints of the Most High. His kingdom is an everlasting kingdom, and all dominions shall serve and obey Him (Dan.7:27).

This is an amazing promise. The Kingdom of God comes to fulfilment when authority and power are given to the saints on earth.

We must not use force to bring in the Kingdom. The Holy Spirit will give it to us, when we are ready to receive it. When we are willing to serve and suffer like Jesus, he will be able to trust us with it. If we try to force it, we will lose it.

We will receive the Kingdom of God when we learn to walk through suffering in the power of the Spirit, so a huge number of Christians may have to suffer and die, before the church is ready to receive the fullness of the Kingdom of God.

Different Kingdom

The Kingdom of God will be the opposite of what people expect.

- Christians will not get the power held by politicians and political powers.
- Christian political parties will not be elected to power.
- Christian leaders will not get to hold the office of Prime Minister or President.
- Christians will not get to tell political leaders what to do.
- Jesus will not rule from a throne in Jerusalem.
- A Christian bureaucracy will not control the world.

The Kingdom of God will not be imposed from the top. Jesus made this clear when James and John asked for the privilege of sitting by his side in his Kingdom.

> Jesus called them together and said, "You know that those who are regarded as rulers of the Gentiles lord it over them, and their high officials exercise authority over them. Not so with you. Instead, whoever wants to become great among you must be your servant (Mark 10:42-43).

There is no place for force and control in the Kingdom. Force and control belong to the kingdoms of the world. They will be swept away during the Time of Distress, so they must not be recreated for the Kingdom of God.

The Kingdom of God is a voluntary kingdom. Coercion and force have no place in it (Matt 26:53). By submitting to the political powers and dying on the cross, Jesus demonstrated a different way of doing Kingdom. Even though he could have called on his Father to send a whole host of angels to his aid, Jesus refused to use force, because he knows that loyalty is not won by force (Matt 26:52-53). His people must follow his example. We will receive his Kingdom through suffering and service, not by military power and political coercion.

Jesus' Kingdom is different from all other kingdoms. No threats! No shouting! No fear! No detailed regulations! No coercion! No force! No security services. No torture of opponents! The Holy Spirit will change hearts to love Jesus, as the church proclaims the gospel. The Holy Spirit is the Kingdom builder.

The Holy Spirit exercises all the awesome power of God, so we can expect him to be successful in all he does. Since he has infinite power, we should expect him to bring the Kingdom of God to victory.

Holy Spirit Kingdom

God's will is done on earth as it is in heaven when people obey the Holy Spirit. That simple idea is the key to the coming of the Kingdom. The Holy Spirit is modest, so he does not boast in the scriptures about what he will do. Christians who know him should understand the significance of his role in bringing in the Kingdom.

The Kingdom comes when God's will is done on earth in the same way as it is done in heaven, so to understand how the Kingdom comes, we need to understand how God's will is done in heaven. Psalm 103:19-21 explains how this works.

- God rules in heaven.
- The angels are waiting to do his bidding.
- When he speaks, they obey his word.
- They gladly do his will, because they love him.

94

When Jesus came to earth, he followed the same pattern. Because he loved the Father, he did what he saw him doing.

> Very truly I tell you, the Son can do nothing by himself; he can do only what he sees his Father doing, because whatever the Father does the Son also does (John 5:19).

Jesus watched the Father, and obeyed his word. By doing God's will on earth, as it is done in heaven, Jesus brought the Kingdom close. The Kingdom will come to fullness on earth in the same way.

- Those who are born again into the Kingdom will be keen to do his bidding.

  > Anyone who loves me will obey my teaching (John 14:23).

- The Holy Spirit hears everything that Jesus and the Father say.

  > He will glorify me because it is from me that he will receive what he will make known to you. All that belongs to the Father is mine… the Spirit will receive from me what he will make known to you (John 16:14-15).

- The Holy Spirit reveals Jesus' will to his people.

  > When he, the Spirit of truth, comes, he will guide you into all the truth. He will not speak on his own; he will speak only what he hears (John 16:13).

When a believer obeys the voice of the Spirit, they do Jesus' will, so the Kingdom of God has come in their life. When a community of Christians obeys the leading of the Spirit, the Kingdom of God has come in their midst. When most of the people on earth believe in Jesus and obey the Holy Spirit, the fullness of the Kingdom will have come.

The Holy Spirit can speak to any person in the universe at any time, so he can guide everyone on earth to do God's will. The Kingdom comes when most people on earth choose to obey the Holy Spirit. We need a revelation of his role in establishing the Kingdom. As more and more people live in obedience to the Spirit, God's will will be done and his Kingdom will come on earth.

Holy Spirits Skills

Before the Kingdom can come, the following must happen.

- The people of the world must hear the gospel of Jesus.

- The people of the world must acknowledge their sin.

- The people of the world must believe in Jesus.

- Christians must be set free from the power of evil.

- Every believer must know God's will for their life.

- Christians must be empowered to obey the Spirit.

- Christians must live in peace with each other.

The Holy Spirit can achieve all these things.

- The Holy Spirit will testify to Jesus in the hearts of people who do not know him. He will reveal Jesus to people who need to know him.
  > When the Counsellor comes, whom I will send to you
  > from the Father... he will testify about me (John 15:26).

- The Holy Spirit can convict people of sin.
  > When he comes, he will convict the world of guilt in
  > regard to sin and righteousness and judgment (John 16:8).

  He can soften the hardest heart. Hardened sinners repent of sin when the Holy Spirit convicts them of sin. Paul was persecuting the church with great hostility, but when the Holy Spirit touched him, he fell on his knees in repentance. If the Holy Spirit could get to Paul, he can get to anyone.

- The Holy Spirit can inspire faith in Jesus.
  > We have the same spirit of faith (2 Cor 4:13).

  He gives those who believe a new heart (John 3:5).

- The Holy Spirit has the power to set his people free from evil.
  > Where the Spirit of the Lord is, there is freedom (2 Cor
  > 3:17).

  > The Spirit who gives life has set you free (Rom 8:2).

- The Holy Spirit can teach believers the truth.

  The Counsellor, the Holy Spirit, whom the Father will send in my name, will teach you all things (John 14:26).

  When he, the Spirit of truth, comes, he will guide you into all truth (John 16:13).

  The Spirit of truth will teach all truth to those who seek the truth.

- The Holy Spirit will empower his people to obey Jesus.

  I tell you the truth, anyone who has faith in me will do what I have been doing. He will do even greater things than these, because I am going to the Father (John 14:12).

- The Holy Spirit can destroy fear and replace it with peace.

  Peace I leave with you; my peace I give you… Do not let your hearts be troubled and do not be afraid (John 14:27).

The Holy Spirit has the ability to bring every person on the earth to faith in Jesus. All he needs is the freedom to act and a body to carry him into the world, so he can flow out and touch those who need him.

Beautiful Kingdom

The Holy Spirit will bring in a beautiful Kingdom. He will work in the hearts of all people to convict them of sin and to testify to Jesus. He will draw all people to Jesus, causing them to be born again. The Holy Spirit will guide them into all truth and teach them how to live. As he produces the fruits of love, peace, patience, kindness and joy, people will begin to care for each other and provide everyone with what they need. Peace on earth will come and our groaning creation will be restored.

The Kingdom created by the Holy Spirit will be a voluntary kingdom. There is no need for force and coercion when the Holy Spirit is free to work (Zech 4:6).

Suffering Releases the Spirit

The Kingdom of God is established by service and suffering. The reason is simple. The Holy Spirit loves service. When Christians serve others, he is there with them, touching the hearts of those they serve. Serving destroys the powers of darkness. When Judas had betrayed Jesus, the political powers gained a victory. Jesus washed Judas's feet to nullify the power of their victory (John 13:1-30).

The Holy Spirit really goes to work when Christians suffer as they serve. Peter explains.

> If you are insulted because of the name of Christ, you are blessed, for the Spirit of glory and of God rests on you (1 Peter 4:14).

Peter is referring back to the Shekinah Glory of God. When we suffer for Jesus, the Holy Spirit rests on us, and flows out to touch those who are persecuting us. When Christians respond with agape love to those who intend them harm, the Holy Spirit has freedom to work in those doing the harm.

When people watch a Christian suffering, they open up to the Holy Spirit. He is able to convict them of sin and reveal Jesus. A good example is the centurion who crucified Jesus.

> When the centurion saw what had happened, he glorified God, saying, "Certainly this was a righteous man!" (Luke 23:47).

This centurion was a battle-hardened killing machine, who had crucified hundreds of people. Yet after watching Jesus die, this man glorified God and declared that Jesus was a righteous man. Jesus' suffering had released the Holy Spirit to work in his heart.

Defeating the Powers

God will defeat the principalities and powers with the church, but the process is not what we expect (Eph 3:10). The powers of evil will not be defeated by force, but suffering. When the church is willing to suffer for Jesus, the Holy Spirit is freed to drive out the evil powers.

The fruit of the Holy Spirit is peace, so peace can overcome anger and wrath (Prov 15:1). When we respond to evil with anger, we stir up more anger, which grieves the Holy Spirit and releases the powers of evil. Spirits of anger and hatred get control of the people that we resist.

Political power cannot defeat evil.

- When we rely on political power, the Holy Spirit flees.
- When we use coercion against evil, he is squeezed out.
- Whenever we resist evil with force, spirits of anger and hatred are empowered.

When Christians take up the cross and follow Jesus, the Holy Spirit is released, and he is able to defeat the principalities and powers.

The Kingdom of God cannot be established by war, because as soon as war starts, the Holy Spirit has to withdraw. This creates a spiritual vacuum, which allows the principalities and powers to move in. War always makes a situation worse, even if the cause appears to be good. The forces of evil gain a stronghold on those who participate in the fighting, which allows them to steal the victory.

The Holy Spirit will win every struggle with the powers of darkness, provided he is given a free hand. When Christians get involved in fighting, he is constrained. When the church commits to suffering, the Holy Spirit is empowered to defeat the powers of evil. Suffering in the face of evil releases the Holy Spirit, allowing him to achieve victory.

False Assumption

The following statements are part of the accepted wisdom.

- We must resist evil, or be overcome by evil.
- Violence must be destroyed, before it destroys us.
- We must defend our way of life, or be forced to surrender our faith.

- We must use force against those who hate the gospel, or it might be lost.
- We must defeat those who want to harm us, before they destroy us.

At the physical level, these statements appear to be true, but at the spiritual level, they are wrong. Violent people often harm good people. Evil nations sometimes invade peaceful nations. However, when we use force to defend our way of life, we may gain a temporary victory, but the Holy Spirit pulls back and the Kingdom of God goes into retreat.

Revelation and Endurance

Commitment to enduring through suffering is a major theme in the Book of Revelation. John understood that endurance through suffering brings in the Kingdom.

> Your brother and companion in the suffering and kingdom
> and patient endurance that are ours in Jesus (Rev 1:9).

Suffering and the Kingdom go together.

John wrote his letters to the seven churches to encourage them to endure through suffering. If we focus on the faults of the churches, we miss something important. Jesus encourages his people to endure suffering during a time when terrible evil has emerged on earth. Most of the letters end with a promise to those who overcome. The church in Laodicea has a dreadful reputation, but Jesus gave it an amazing promise.

> To him who overcomes, I will give the right to sit with me
> on my throne, just as I overcame and sat down with my
> Father on his throne. He who has an ear, let him hear
> what the Spirit says to the churches (Rev 3:21-22).

This is an important promise. Christians who persevere through suffering sit with Jesus at the right hand of God.

Evil is defeated by the cross. The Holy Spirit will bring in the Kingdom through a church that endures suffering during a time of great evil.

> They overcame him by the blood of the Lamb and by the
> word of their testimony; they did not love their lives so
> much as to shrink from death (Rev 12:11).

This seems like a paradox, but the people of the Lamb experience victory, when they are willing to die for their faith. Patient endurance frees the Holy Spirit to destroy evil.

Church Almost Destroyed

During the Time of Distress, persecution will almost destroy the church. John saw a vision of two witnesses, two lampstands and two olive trees, which represent a truncated church and a restrained Holy Spirit. In the latter part of this vision, the political powers persecute the church so severely, that it appears to be dead.

> When they have finished their testimony, the beast that
> comes up from the Abyss will attack them, and overpower
> and kill them (Rev 11:7).

The people of the world celebrate joyously because a minor irritant is gone (Rev 11:10) but God has a surprise for the world. When the church appears to be dead, he breathes the life of the Spirit onto it and raises it up to victory.

> The breath of life from God entered them, and they stood on
> their feet, and terror struck those who saw them (Rev 11:11).

A radical church that has survived and prepared where no one is looking will burst onto the world stage. The people of the world will be shocked when they realise that church is not dead, but has been made powerful through suffering.

Bride of Christ

The book of Revelation climaxes with the Holy Spirit giving the Kingdom to a church that has learned to serve and suffer. The suffering church is described as a bride.

> Let us rejoice and be glad and give him glory! For the
> wedding of the Lamb has come, and his bride has made
> herself ready (Rev 19:7).

Heaven and earth are waiting for the time when the bride has prepared herself. Those who belong to the bride are blessed.

> Then the angel said to me, "Write this: Blessed are those who are invited to the wedding supper of the Lamb!" And he added, "These are the true words of God" (Rev 19:9).

The next scene is not the second coming, but a description of the Kingdom of God coming on earth, as the enemies of the Kingdom are defeated by the power of God (Rev 19:11-21). The Bride does not prepare for the second coming of Jesus. She prepares to receive the Kingdom as a gift from the Holy Spirit (keyword: Heavenly Army). The Bride is wearing fine linen.

> Fine linen, bright and clean, was given her to wear. (Fine linen stands for the righteous acts of God's holy people) (Rev 19:8).

The meaning of the white linen given to the saints had been explained earlier in the fifth seal.

> When he opened the fifth seal, I saw under the altar the souls of those who had been slain because of the word of God and the testimony they had maintained... Then each of them was given a white robe, and they were told to wait a little longer, until the full number were killed just as they had been (Rev 6:9,11).

White garments represent persecution for obedience to Jesus. This persecution begins after the opening of the first four seals and ends when the Spirit gives them the Kingdom. The number that will suffer through this persecution is immense.

> After this I looked and there before me was a great multitude that no one could count, from every nation, tribe, people and language, standing before the throne and in front of the Lamb. They were wearing white robes (Rev 7:9).

John saw a huge multitude in white robes willing to sacrifice their lives for Jesus, so his Kingdom can come on earth.

> Then one of the elders asked me, "These in white robes— who are they, and where did they come from?" I answered, "Sir, you know." And he said, "These are they who have come out of the great tribulation; they have washed their robes and made them white in the blood of the Lamb" (Rev 7:13-14).

A great multitude will suffer through this persecution and enter into the victory of the Kingdom.

God cannot bring in this time of suffering until the bride is willing to go through it.

> The Spirit and the bride say, "Come!" And let him who hears say, "Come" (Rev 22:17)!

When the bride is ready, she says, "Come", because she is ready and willing to pass through a Time of Distress to enter the Kingdom of God. She does not cry out, "Rescue me!" Holy Spirit is waiting for a church that is willing to suffer until his work is complete without pleading to be rescued.

Christian Community

During this time of suffering, the religious structures of the church will be torn down and destroyed. Communities defined by love and service will emerge in their place, as Christians are forced into deeper relationships with each other. They will have been forced together in order to survive. In many places, this will be the only way that Christians can survive through the worst darkness.

Small groups who trust each other will get ready by buying or renting homes close together, so they can support each other. The Holy Spirit will flood them with love and power, as they get serious about Jesus new commandment.

> As I have loved you, so you must love one another (John 13:34).

These Christians will form communities that transform their neighbourhoods. When the structures of society begin to fall apart, they will work out alternative ways of sustaining life.

Multiply and Grow

Many will see the benefits of belonging to a Christian community and want to join. Provided they commit to the ethos of love and service, people will be welcome, whether they are Christians or not. Some people who have lived in a Christian community for a while and understand how it functions will go out and help Christians in other neighbourhoods to get started where they live. The number of kingdom communities will grow quickly as the new way of living spreads from place to place (keyword: Community).

Each of these Christian communities will be a microcosm of the Kingdom of God. They will provide everything that modern governments have failed to provide. The difference is that they will flow out of love and service, without any need for coercion. A new way of living will spread through society in the same way as yeast spreads through dough.

> The kingdom of heaven is like yeast that a woman took and mixed into about sixty pounds of flour until it worked all through the dough (Matt 13:33).

The Holy Spirit will mix the Kingdom through society by moving from neighbourhood to neighbourhood (keyword: Tens and Hundreds).

Voluntary Communities

Participation in a kingdom community will be voluntary. A person joining will have to acknowledge the leadership that is in place, but they will be able to withdraw their submission at any time, if they do not like what the leaders are doing. If they think the leadership has turned sour, they will be free to leave the community and join another.

The leaders of a community will only have as much authority as the members give to them. If they are trusted, they will be given authority to organise some of the activities in their neighbourhood. If they are not trusted, they will not be able to do much. The leaders will understand that more can be achieved by love and service than through control.

Kingdom communities will be held together by love and compassion, worked out in sharing and service. People joining a community will have to accept the authority of its leaders, because the benefits from being part of a strong community will far outweigh the loss of freedom.

Fulfilment of Blessing

All God's promises will reach their fulfilment through the Holy Spirit working in the church. Our commission to make disciples of all nations will be successful. Our mandate to fill the earth and manage it will be completed.

> For the earth will be filled with the knowledge of the glory of the Lord, as the waters cover the sea (Hab 2:14).

God's glory will be revealed as his Kingdom fills the earth.

The prophet Micah spoke of the glory of the Kingdom of God. He described it as a time of great peace and blessing.

> They will beat their swords into plowshares and their spears into pruning hooks. Nation will not take up sword against nation, nor will they train for war any more. Every man will sit under his own vine and under his own fig tree, and no one will make them afraid (Mic 4:3-4).

The coming of the Kingdom will bring peace to the whole earth. No one will be poor, and there will be nothing to fear. A season of great blessing will fall upon the earth.

Isaiah's Promise

Isaiah gave a wonderful promise.

> Never again will there be in it an infant who lives but a few days, or an old man who does not live out his years; the one who dies at a hundred will be thought a mere child; the one who fails to reach a hundred will be considered accursed. They will build houses and dwell in them; they will plant vineyards and eat their fruit. No longer will they build houses and others live in them, or plant and others eat. For as the days of a tree, so will be the days of my people; my chosen ones will long enjoy the work of their hands. They will not labor in vain, nor will they bear children doomed to misfortune; for they will be a people blessed by the Lord, they and their descendants with them. Before they call I will answer; while they are still speaking I will hear. The wolf and the lamb will feed together, and the lion will eat straw like the ox, and dust will be the serpent's food. They will neither harm nor destroy on all my holy mountain (Is 65:20-25).

This prophecy is so wonderful that most Christians assume it describes eternal life, but people are still dying, so it must refer to life on this earth. The prophecy reveals the amazing change that the Holy Spirit will bring on earth.

- Sickness defeated;
- Long and full life;
- Productive capital for everyone;
- Prosperous economy;
- Poverty gone;
- Secure and safe homes;
- No crime;
- Blessed by God;
- Animal world transformed;
- Peace replaces aggression.

Sin is the only obstacle to this vision. Jesus dealt to sin on the cross, so we should expect the Holy Spirit to eliminate the effects of sin and restore blessing on earth.

> The LORD will be king over the whole earth. On that day there will be one LORD, and his name the only name (Zech 14:9).

Creation Restored

Paul explained that the earth is crying out for restoration.

> We know that the whole creation has been groaning as in the pains of childbirth right up to the present time (Rom 8:22).

God created a beautiful world, but it was corrupted and distorted when human sin allowed the devil to implement his destructive plans.

> For the creation was subjected to frustration, not by its own choice, but by the will of the one who subjected it (Rom 8:20).

The power of evil was destroyed by the cross. As more and more people believe in Jesus, the Spirit will gain the freedom to restore the earth from the harm done by evil.

> For the creation waits in eager expectation for the children of God to be revealed (Rom 8:19).

106

When most of the people on earth believe in Jesus, it will get close to the state it was in before the fall.

> The creation itself will be liberated from its bondage to decay and brought into the freedom and glory of the children of God (Rom 8:21).

As the Kingdom progresses and faith increases, the Holy Spirit will roll back the effects of sin and restore the creation to its original beauty.

The Holy City

John saw the Holy City coming down from God.

> And he carried me away in the Spirit to a mountain great and high, and showed me the Holy City, Jerusalem, coming down out of heaven from God (Rev 21:10).

This vision is not eternal life, because the nations and kings are still in existence. They will have no place in eternity (Rev 21:24). The Holy City coming down from heaven is a picture of the church receiving the Kingdom of God.

> It shone with the glory of God, and its brilliance was like that of a very precious jewel (Rev 21:11).

If the church is being battered and persecuted on earth, it shines like a precious jewel when seen from a heavenly perspective.

> The nations will walk by its light, and the kings of the earth will bring their splendor into it (Rev 21:24).

The rulers of the nations will submit to Jesus and surrender their authority to those who walk in the light of his Spirit.

As the gospel advances, the curse of sin will fade.

> No longer will there be any curse (Rev 22:3).

The Holy Spirit will break the power of sin that has contaminated the creation. As sin is eliminated, creation will experience an amazing restoration.

> Then the angel showed me the river of the water of life, as clear as crystal, flowing from the throne of God and of the Lamb (Rev 22:1).

The river is the Holy Spirit.

> On each side of the river stood the tree of life, bearing twelve
> crops of fruit, yielding its fruit every month. And the leaves of
> the tree are for the healing of the nations (Rev 22:2).

The fullness of the Kingdom will restore the blessing that existed in the Garden of Eden.

How Long

How long will the season of the Kingdom last? The Bible does not say. The Times of the Gentiles went on for 2000 years, so the Kingdom of God should last at least as long, or much longer. This is God's best season and there is no suggestion in the scriptures that he will cut it short.

When history is complete, the number of people in heaven will be a multitude too big to be counted.

> I looked, and there before me was a great multitude that
> no one could count, from every nation, tribe, people and
> language (Rev 7:9).

The angels have been counted.

> Then I looked and heard the voice of many angels,
> numbering thousands upon thousands, and ten thousand
> times ten thousand (Rev 5:11).

The number of angels is immense, so the number of Christians will eventually be far greater. A vast number of people must come to faith before this promise is fulfilled.

Since the time of Jesus, several billion people have come to faith in him, far short of the multitude that John was promised. History will have to go on for much longer for this countless multitude to be brought in.

If the world were to end now, the number of people lost would far exceed those who are saved. This score makes God seem quite mean, as the vast majority of people who have lived on earth would go to eternal destruction. This impression is wrong, because it judges God's performance on the first half of the game, when half the team is missing and the coach is seriously constrained.

By the time the game is complete, the score will have changed dramatically. During the second half, most of those who live on earth will be saved and only a minority lost. The second half could be five times longer than the first half, so the total saved will be enormous. The few billion people lost during the Times of the Gentiles will be minute compared to the thousands of billions that will come to Jesus in the future. The final score will be far more respectable, and better reflect God's character.

God is gracious and generous, so he will not be stingy with salvation. He will allow history to continue for long enough to ensure that the number saved will vastly exceed the number who are lost.

God promised at least five times that he is faithful to a thousand generations (Deut 7:9, 1 Chron 16:15).

> He remembers his covenant forever, the promise he made,
> for a thousand generations (Ps 105:8).

Some numbers in scriptures are figurative, but if any number should be taken literally, surely this is it. For God to keep this covenant promise, a thousand generations will have to live on earth (keyword: Not Millennium).

A new generation is born every twenty years, so we have had about 500 generations since the time of Abraham. This means that another 500 generations would have to live on earth for this promise to be fulfilled. That will take another 10,000 years, which is just long enough to get thousands of billions of people into God's Kingdom.

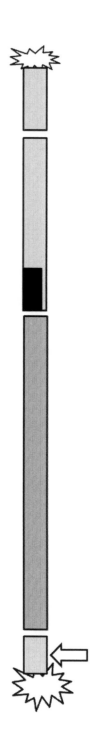

11

Little Season

Man of Lawlessness

The epochal event that marks the end of the Times of the Kingdom is the Man of Lawlessness. Paul describes this man in his letter to the Thessalonians. They had been unsettled by prophecies and false rumours. Paul explains that Jesus will not appear until after "the rebellion".

> Don't let anyone deceive you in any way, for that day will not come until the rebellion occurs and the *man of lawlessness* is revealed, the man doomed to destruction (2 Thes 2:3).

An evil man called the Man of Lawlessness will lead a rebellion against God's law at the end of the age. He will be destroyed by the Appearance of Jesus.

As his name suggests, this man rebels against God's law. He will scoff at God's justice and advocate the restoration of human government to bring "proper" justice. Many who feel aggrieved will join him in agitating for change. This man is held back until the proper time.

> You know what is holding him back, so that he may be revealed at the proper time. For the secret power of lawlessness is already at work; but the one who now holds it back will continue to do so till he is taken out of the way (2 Thes 2:6-7).

The Holy Spirit holds back the power of lawlessness. At the end of the age, he will release his restraint on evil and allow the Man of Lawlessness to emerge.

Deceptive

When he emerges the Man of Lawlessness will appear to be wise and good, but his true nature will soon be exposed.

> The coming of the lawless one will be in accordance with the work of Satan displayed in all kinds of counterfeit miracles, signs and wonders, and every sort of evil that deceives those who are perishing (2 Thes 2:9-10).

These, signs and wonders refer to his attempt to improve society using political power and human government.

Lawlessness is not the absence of law. Lawlessness is rejecting God's law and replacing it with human laws. The Man of Lawlessness will claim that the world has changed and that God's law is not sufficiently sophisticated to be a basis for justice in a modern world. He will advocate a return to democracy as a superior form of government. People who feel maligned by God's justice will join him in his efforts to establish new laws using democratic processes.

Some people who appear to be living righteous lives will begin delighting in unrighteousness, but this will make them vulnerable to deception (2 Thes 2:12).

> They refused to love the truth and so be saved. For this reason God sends them a powerful delusion so that they will believe the lie (2 Thes 2:10-11).

These people will stop trusting in Jesus' salvation and will begin to believe the lie of power politics. This lie has been discredited during the Time of Distress, but the passing of time will allow it to take hold again. The Man of Lawlessness will stir up discontent and instigate a rebellion against God.

Not Antichrist

The Man of Lawlessness should not be called the Antichrist. He is a political leader, whereas an antichrist is someone who denies Jesus (1 John 2:22). The Man of Lawlessness must not be confused with the Beast of Revelation. The Beast is a powerful nation, whereas the Man of Lawlessness is a political leader. They operate in different seasons. The Beast rises to power during the Time of Distress, whereas the Man of Lawlessness is closely linked with the Appearance of Jesus.

> The lawless one will be revealed, whom the Lord Jesus will overthrow with the breath of his mouth and destroy by the splendour of his appearance (2 Thes 2:8).

Jesus will overthrow the Man of Lawlessness on the day of his Appearance (keyword: Not Antichrist).

> This will happen when the Lord Jesus is revealed from heaven in blazing fire with his powerful angels (2 Thes 1:7).

Satan Bound

The season ushered by the Man of Lawlessness is called the "little season" or "short time" The passage that describes this season is not well understood.

> And I saw an angel coming down out of heaven, having the key to the Abyss and holding in his hand a great chain. He seized the dragon, that ancient serpent, who is the devil, or Satan, and bound him for a thousand years. He threw him into the Abyss, and locked and sealed it over him, to keep him from deceiving the nations anymore until the thousand years were ended. After that, he must be set free for a **short time** (Rev 20:1-3).

The binding of the devil is not a future event. The devil was totally defeated by Jesus' victory on the cross.

> Having disarmed the powers and authorities, he made a public spectacle of them, triumphing over them by the cross (Col 2:15).

Jesus proved that he had destroyed the devil's power by casting out demons (Matt 12:29). Since he has ascended into heaven, Jesus has worked on earth through his body. The victory won on the cross must now be enforced on earth by the Holy Spirit working through the church.

Jesus gave responsibility for binding the powers of evil to his disciples.

> Whatever you bind on earth will be bound in heaven, and whatever you loose on earth will be loosed in heaven (Matt 18:18).

He repeated this challenge to stress its importance (Matt 16:19). God's people have responsibility for enforcing the binding of evil.

During the Times of the Gentiles, the church does not use this authority very effectively, so evil continues to operate as though it had never been bound. The Kingdom of God comes to fulfilment when the Church gets to grips with this authority and binds the powers of evil. When the church is on the top of its game, the devil is bound and powerless.

John said that the devil is bound for a thousand years (Rev 20:3). This is not a literal time. A thousand equals ten to the power of three. Ten represents completeness and three is perfection, so a thousand equals perfect completeness. The thousand years describes the season when the Kingdom of God has perfect fulfilment. This time may last for much longer than a thousand years, but throughout the season, the devil is totally bound (keyword: Not Millennium).

Lost Place

The book of Revelation describes reality as it appears from heaven. From that perspective, the devil was bound and destroyed by the cross. People with an earthly perspective find it hard to believe that the devil has been defeated. This allows him to keep working as if the cross has failed. John refers to this as being cast down on the earth, because the devil is allowed to operate according to an earthly perspective, rather than the heavenly one.

The casting down of the devil is described most clearly in John's vision of the woman and the male child (Rev 12). When Jesus arrived in heaven, Satan's power is gone.

> And there was war in heaven. Michael and his angels
> fought against the dragon, and the dragon and his angels
> fought back. But he was not strong enough, and they lost
> their place in heaven (Rev 12:7-8).

The devil gained his authority as an "accuser" (Rev 12:10). Because all have sinned, he had a great deal of authority and a "place in heaven". Once Jesus had paid the penalty for sin, he could no longer accuse God's people.

> They overcame him by the blood of the Lamb and by the
> word of their testimony (Rev 12:11).

He lost his place in heaven.

> The accuser of our brothers, who accuses them before our
> God day and night, has been hurled down (Rev 12:10).

There was great rejoicing in heaven, because this defeat opened the way for the saints to receive his Kingdom.

> salvation and the power and the kingdom of our God, and
> the authority of his Christ..... Therefore rejoice, you
> heavens and you who dwell in them (Rev 12:10,12).

Those who operate in the heavenly realms know that evil has been defeated. Unfortunately, those who see things from the earthly perspective allow him to continue working.

> Woe to the earth and the sea, because the devil has gone
> down to you! He is filled with fury, because he knows that
> his *time is short* (Rev 12:12).

He desperately clings to power by preventing people from seeing Jesus victory from the heavenly perspective.

Devil Unbound

The Kingdom of God will continue until the full numbers of people have come to faith. When all God's promises and purposes have been fulfilled on earth, he will set in train the series of events that bring in the next season. The devil and his forces will be released for one last time.

> When the thousand years are over, Satan will be released
> from his prison (Rev 20:7).

He does not escape, but is released by the Holy Spirit to achieve a divine purpose.

God demonstrates his infinite mercy by giving Satan one last chance to redeem himself. He was created by God for a special purpose, but fell from his exalted position and became the enemy of good. Despite the terrible harm he has done to the world, God will give him one last chance to fulfil his calling before the end of the age. He will never be able to accuse God of not being gracious.

The devil will not take the opportunity given to him, but will go out to do evil by getting control of the nations again.

> He will go out to deceive the nations in the four corners of the earth—Gog and Magog—and to gather them for battle. In number, they are like the sand on the seashore (Rev 20:8).

To score a victory over Jesus, he will stir up rebellion among the nations. He is not creative, so he just uses the same lies about God that he used at the beginning. People all over the world will join this rebellion. "Gog and Magog" is a reference to many nations rebelling against God.

The rebellion will begin with people grumbling about the Kingdom of God. They will spread lies about the Christian influence in society in an attempt to undermine the church.

> They marched across the breadth of the earth and surrounded the camp of God's people, the city he loves (Rev 20:9).

This is not a literal war. The camp of God's people represents all the people in the world who have chosen to follow Jesus. The beloved city is the Kingdom of God. Gog and Magog represent worldwide opposition to God. Those who come under the devil's power will begin to persecute the church.

Persecution will be a new experience for the Christians living through this season. Most will be unprepared. Those who do not understand that God has released the devil will be shocked by the rapid deterioration of the spiritual climate. Fortunately, this season of rebellion will be quite brief.

After that, he must be set free for a **short time** (Rev 20:3).

As the Kingdom goes on, the memory of earlier seasons when evil prevailed will grow dim. Some Christians will find it hard to believe that Satan and his angels are truly evil. Some will consider that Satan and his followers have been treated harshly by God.

This brief season at the end of history will reveal the true character of evil. The people of the world will get a brief taste of its horrors. After this experience, it will be obvious that the devil and his followers deserve their fate (Rev 20:10).

Fire from Heaven

The devil will succeed in building support, but he will not achieve his objective.

> But fire came down from heaven and devoured them (Rev 20:9).

This fire from heaven is not literal. The event that follows the fire is the last judgment, so this must be a reference to the Appearance of Jesus (Rev 20:11-15). This is confirmed in Paul's letter to the Thessalonians.

> When the Lord Jesus is revealed from heaven in blazing fire with his powerful angels, he will punish those who do not know God and do not obey the gospel of our Lord Jesus (2 Thes 1:7-8).

The blazing fire is the appearance of Jesus.

> Then the lawless one will be revealed, whom the Lord Jesus will overthrow with the breath of his mouth and destroy by the splendor of his **appearing** (2 Thes 2:8).

The Man of Lawlessness and his followers will be destroyed by the splendour of Jesus' appearance.

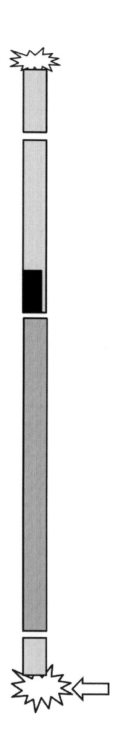

12

Jesus Appearance

The short season that marks the end of the Kingdom age will be cut short when Jesus appears on the stage. This event is often referred to as the "second coming", but this phrase is not used in the scriptures, so I will not use it. The Greek word "parousia" means "appearance" or "arrival". It is a much stronger word than "erchomai," the usual Greek word for "come". The epochal event that marks the end of history is the Appearance of Jesus (Parousia).

The Bible says that his appearance will light up the sky from one end to the other. Those who believe in him will share in his glory. The first half of Matthew 24 refers to the destruction of Jerusalem, but Jesus inserted a brief description of his Appearance by way of contrast.

> For as lightning that comes from the east is visible even in the west, so will be the appearance (parousia) of the Son of Man (Matt 24:27).

No one will miss this event. Jesus will be visible to everyone on earth, like a great flash of lightening. A good analogy would be a rock star waiting in the wings while the atmosphere builds. The entrance onto the stage in a climax of sound and light would be called an "appearance".

Spiritual Interjection

The Appearance of Jesus is a massive interjection of the spiritual dimension into our physical world. It is difficult to describe in human words, so we should be careful when interpreting the bible passages that describe it. The popular teaching that Jesus will come down like a bungee jumper on a skyhook is misleading. The common idea that a crowd of Christian skyrockets will shoot into the sky fails to understand the reality that we live in.

We tend to think of heaven and earth as two different places. Heaven is up there, earth is down here, and a huge gap is in between. This gap is real, but the assumption that these two worlds are far apart is wrong. We live in a multi-dimensional universe in which the spiritual dimensions exist in parallel to the three-dimensional physical world. Angels can move between the spiritual and physical dimensions, but humans only see the physical side of existence.

At the ascension, Jesus appeared to go up into the air and behind a cloud. He was not an interstellar rocket man shooting for a far distant planet, but was moving back into the spiritual realms from which he had come. Because the eyes of the disciples were calibrated to see the physical world, he seemed to go into the sky and disappear. If they could have seen with spiritual eyes, they would have realised that he had simply moved across the divide into the spiritual realms.

In the same way, Jesus appears again when our seeing changes. The spiritual realms are currently hidden from the people on earth, but they will be opened up for everyone to see. Paul wrote of the "manifestation of Jesus' appearance" (2 Thes 2:8). He was explaining that the spiritual dimensions will be blown open and be visible to everyone on earth.

The limits of our human seeing make the physical world appear bright and real. The spiritual dimension seems distant and dim to us, as it must be perceived by faith. When our seeing is changed, the physical world will fade into obscurity. As the spiritual world comes into clearer focus, we will be stunned by its glory. Jesus does not come back to earth. He appears when the spiritual world is opened and joined with the physical world for everyone to see.

Heaven Opened

Before Jesus was born as a baby, he existed with the Father and the Spirit in the spiritual realms.

> He was with God in the beginning (John 1:2).

He left the spiritual realms behind when he became human.

> He made himself nothing by taking the very nature of a servant, being made in human likeness (Phil 2:7).

After his resurrection, Jesus returned to the spiritual realms from which he had come (Acts 2:32-33; Phil 2:9).

> God raised Christ from the dead and seated him at his right hand in the spiritual realms (Eph 1:20).

When our spiritual eyes are opened to see clearly, the spiritual dimensions of life will suddenly be real. When the curtain is pulled back, the indescribable glory of Jesus will be revealed. Once they can see reality clearly, everyone on earth will see Jesus seated on the throne at the right hand of the Father. He has always been there, but from a human perspective, he will seem to have appeared.

Second Resurrection

Human eyes will be opened to see into the spiritual world at the second resurrection. There are two resurrections. John distinguished between these two events in his gospel. The first resurrection is for those who believe.

> I tell you the truth, whoever hears my word and believes him who sent me has eternal life and will not be condemned; he has crossed over from death to life. I tell you the truth, a time is coming and has now come when the dead will hear the voice of the Son of God and those who hear will live (John 5:24-25).

121

The first resurrection is not a future event. It occurs when we are born again to new life by faith in Jesus. Those who are baptised into Christ, have not just died with him, they are raised with him (Rom 6:1-10).

> Having been buried with him in baptism and raised with him through your faith in the power of God....God made you alive with Christ (Col 2:12-13).

This verse is past tense. Christians are united with Jesus in his death and resurrection. Those who believe have died with him and are raised to new life in him.

John also described the first resurrection in his vision.

> I saw thrones on which were seated those who had been given authority to judge.... They came to life and reigned with Christ a thousand years...This is the first resurrection (Rev 20:4-5).

In the spiritual dimension, all Christians have been raised to life in Jesus and rule with him. We do not get this, but John did. He called it the first resurrection. It is a spiritual resurrection that only affects those who believe in Jesus.

The first resurrection gives new spiritual life to believers, while those outside Christ continue to be spiritually dead. The second resurrection is a general resurrection of everyone that occurs at the end of the age before the last judgment. John described this event in his gospel (keyword: Judgment).

> Do not be amazed at this, for a time is coming when all who are in their graves will hear his voice and come out-- those who have done good will rise to live, and those who have done evil will rise to be condemned (John 5:28-29).

John described the same event in his final vision.

> The rest of the dead did not come to life until the thousand years were ended (Rev 20:5).

The second resurrection leads to the final judgment.

> And I saw the dead, great and small, standing before the throne, and books were opened... The sea gave up the dead that were in it, and death and Hades gave up the dead that were in them... (Rev 20:12-13).

The first resurrection enabled Christians to see by faith. The second resurrection enables everyone to see into the spiritual world in the same way that we now see the physical world. It does not change the universe, but dramatically changes the way that people see it.

When the last trumpet sounds, everyone will be able to see as John could see during his vision. After the second resurrection, all people will be able to see what John saw.

> Then I saw a Lamb, looking as if it had been slain, standing at the center of the throne (Rev 5:6).

Jesus has been on this throne since his ascension. At the general resurrection, everyone will see him there.

All Changed

Paul explained to the Corinthians how we will be changed at the last trumpet.

> Listen, I tell you a mystery: We will not all sleep, but we will all be changed—in a flash, in the twinkling of an eye, at the last trumpet. For the trumpet will sound, the dead will be raised imperishable, and we will be changed (1 Cor 15:51-52).

When the angel sounds the last trumpet, we will be changed. The previous verse describes part of this change.

> And just as we have worn the image of the earthly man, so shall we wear the image of the heavenly man (1 Cor 15:49).

We now live with all the constraints of earthly people. We can only see the spiritual dimension of life through the eyes of faith. When we are changed to be like heavenly people, we will be able to see the spiritual world as well. In a twinkling of an eye, the spiritual and the physical world will be merged into one reality. That will change everything.

The Appearance of Jesus is the effect of the second resurrection. Everyone who has ever lived will be raised to life and be able to see both the spiritual world and the physical world. All things will have come together.

Great Gaze

When Jesus ascended into heaven from the Mount of Olives, near Bethany, his disciples stood watching as he disappeared behind the clouds. An angel spoke to them and said,

> Why do ye stand gazing into the heaven? This Jesus who was received from you into the heaven, shall so come in the same way as you gazed on him going into heaven (Acts 1:11).

We assume that the angel was saying that Jesus would return in the same way that he departed; by coming down from behind a cloud. This is not quite correct. The angel said that the "gazing" would be the same. The disciples were gazing into the spiritual world, but seeing nothing. The angel was promising that Jesus would appear when people are able to gaze into the spiritual realms and see. The Appearance of Jesus occurs when people are changed so that they can see correctly into both the physical and spiritual worlds.

We assume that Jesus must return to earth to appear, but this is not correct. When the veil that prevents us from seeing the spiritual dimension of life is removed, he will suddenly appear to everyone. He will not have moved, but will seem to have returned to earth again.

Although we were already seated in heaven with Jesus, those who believe will feel like they have been taken up to be with him. Those who do not believe in Jesus will see him in all his glory. As he appears in glory for the first time, it will seem like he has come right down to earth.

Earth and Sky

The appearance of the earth and sky will be totally changed by the second resurrection. With the physical and spiritual dimensions merged, earth will seem much less grand. We look at the stars in the sky and are filled with wonder. Pictures of the earth taken from space make the earth seem amazing. However, once we see the glory of the spiritual realms, the physical world will shrivel into insignificance.

Earth and sky will seem to collapse and disappear. Physical things will not have changed, but we will be seeing them in correct perspective for the first time. We think that space is immense, but when we see the spiritual realms, it will suddenly seem small. As we see the glory of the spiritual realms for the first time, earth and space will shrink away.

Some of this is captured in this woodenly literal translation of Peter's prophecy.

> The day of the Lord will come like a thief. The spiritual world will come near with a booming, the orderly arrangement of things will be loosed by fire, and the earth and everything in it will be exposed…. That day will bring about the releasing of the spiritual dimensions by fire, and the order of things will liquefy in the heat (2 Pet 3:10,12).

The elements will seem to be dissolving before our eyes. The stars will seem to be rolling up like a scroll. They will not be disappearing, but the beauty and wonder of the spiritual realms is so wonderful, that the earth and sky, as we know them, will fade into insignificance. Such a dramatic event will produce plenty of heat and light.

John saw the same events when heaven was opened to him.

> Then I saw a great white throne and him who was seated on it. The earth and the heavens fled from his presence, and there was no place for them (Rev 20:11).

When Jesus is revealed, earth and sky shrink into nothing.

Great Separation

People who have not been born again will be almost destroyed by the sight of Jesus. Evil has only been able to survive because it has been shielded from the spiritual realms. Once the spiritual and the physical are brought together, evil will be blown away in a great separation.

> That is how it will be at the appearance (parousia) of the Son of Man. Two men will be in the field; one will be taken and the other left. Two women will be grinding with a hand mill; one will be taken and the other left (Matt 24:39-41).

From the human perspective, Christians and non-Christians often seem to be working alongside each other. When we see clearly into the spiritual dimensions of reality, we will realise that we are actually living and working in a separate existence. It will seem like we have been pushed apart.

Last Judgment
The appearance of Jesus leads to the last judgment.

> I saw the dead, great and small, standing before the throne, and books were opened. Another book was opened, which is the book of life. The dead were judged according to what they had done as recorded in the books. The sea gave up the dead that were in it, and death and Hades gave up the dead that were in them, and each person was judged according to what they had done (Rev 20:12-13).

Death will be destroyed forever.

> Then death and Hades were thrown into the lake of fire. The lake of fire is the second death (Rev 20:14).

> The last enemy to be destroyed is death (1 Cor 15:26).

As heaven and earth merge, Christians will experience the joy of eternal life in the presence of Jesus (keyword: Eternity).

> For what is our hope, our joy, or the crown in which we will glory in the presence of our Lord Jesus (1 Thes 2:19)?

> You will be blameless and holy in the presence of our God and Father (1 Thes 3:13).

Those who have rejected Jesus will go to eternal destruction.

> They will be punished with everlasting destruction and shut out from the presence of the Lord and from the glory of his might on the day he appears (2 Thes 1:9-10).

People not born again of the Spirit will be destroyed, because there is no place in the universe where they can survive (keyword: Eternal Destruction).

Surprise
Everyone on earth will be surprised by Jesus' Appearance.

> The day of the Lord will come like a thief in the night. While people are saying, "Peace and safety," destruction will come on them suddenly (1 Thes 5:2-3).

Just as there is no advance warning when a thief strikes, so there will be no warning of Jesus' appearance.

Many Christians claim to know the timing of Jesus' appearance. He warned that there would be no preliminary signs.

> But about that day or hour no one knows, not even the angels in heaven, nor the Son, but only the Father (Matt 24:36).

There is no point in trying to second-guess Jesus. Christians should be ready at all times, so we will not be embarrassed when he appears.

> Therefore, keep watch, because you do not know on what day your Lord will come... So you also must be ready, because the Son of Man will come at an hour when you do not expect him (Matt 24:42,44).

Those who do Jesus' will, will be ready whenever he appears.

Handing over the Kingdom

History climaxes when Jesus hands back to his Father the Kingdom that the Holy Spirit has given to the church. He does not return to establish his Kingdom. Jesus appears when the Kingdom is complete.

> But each in turn: Christ, the firstfruits; then, when he appears (parousia), those who belong to him. Then the end will come, when he hands over the kingdom to God the Father after he has destroyed all dominion, authority and power... For he must reign until he has put all his enemies under his feet (1 Cor 15:23-25).

Jesus reigns in heaven until the Holy Spirit, working through the suffering church, has overcome all opposition to the gospel (Psalm 110:1). When his Kingdom has come to fullness and run its course, Jesus will appear to bring all things to an end. He then hands the Kingdom back to God the Father, so he can get his next project underway.

> Then the Son himself will be made subject to him who put everything under him, so that God may be all in all (1 Cor 15:28).

Creative Future

The consummation of the Kingdom on earth will not be the end of all things. God will not go into retirement and rest forever. He started his action on earth by placing people in a garden, with instructions to push out and fill the entire earth. Having achieved the fulfilment of his Kingdom on earth, he will want to push out and fill the entire universe. The spiritual and physical dimensions will continue to be integrated and a few extra dimensions may be added. I presume that those who have learned to serve Jesus during life on earth will continue to work with him to fill the universe with wonderful worlds and kingdoms.

By the same author

Being Church Where We Live

This challenging book offers a radical vision for the church that will stir hearts and provide guidance for people living through the Time of Distress and preparing for the glory of the Kingdom.

Coming Soon

The Government of God

The Kingdom of God is one of the greatest themes of the Bible. This book will explain how the government of God can transform economic and social life.

The Prophetic Ministry

The church urgently needs the release of the prophetic ministry. These study notes describe the operation of this important ministry.

Christian Healing

Fifteen keys that will help God's people obtain victory over pain and sickness.

About the author

Ron McKenzie is a Christian writer
living in Christchurch, New Zealand.
During the 1980s, he served as
the pastor of a church,
but found that he did not fit that role.
He is now employed as an economist
and writes in his spare time.
He is married with three adult children.